GLOBAL
GIRLS

Compiled by Karen Gee

Edited by Chelsea Wilcox

Typeset in Minion Pro 12.5/18pt

 A catalogue record for this
work is available from the
National Library of Australia

National Library of Australia Catalogue-in-Publication data:
Global Girls/Karen Gee

ISBN: 978-0-6454374-2-3 (Hardback)

ISBN: 978-0-6454374-3-0 (Ebook)

CONTENTS

INTRODUCTION
BY KAREN GEE

They say that women who support women are more successful. It is a proven fact that women in particular benefit from collaboration over competition. I believe the game changer lies with putting yourself in environments that give you the opportunity to surround yourself with positive, like-minded women, who want to support and encourage each other's journeys in the workplace and home life. Meaningful connections will last a lifetime. Solid relationships allow you to connect on another level and allow you to go out and be your best.

Shine Theory is a practice of mutual investment with the simple premise that, 'I don't shine if you don't shine,' first started by Ann Friedman and Aminatou Sow. The theory is practiced when relationships are charaterised by uplifting and supporting, rather than by comparing or tearing down others, when friends see the mutual value, and come together to support one another.

That brings me to the introduction of this book. I wanted to bring together women with no certain criteria, women who wanted to be supported by other women, and in turn, inspire each other to place value on oneself. Through the Karen Gee brand, I have built some wonderful relationships with women – ladies that I am in awe of, who are so talented and inspiring – and thought, *Why not bring as many women together as I can to support one another?* So Global Girls was born. Women throughout the world, different careers, different stages of life, all facing great happiness, as well as challenges along the way. The idea was that we are unique in our own right, however, together are powerful. We connect most days, usually sharing the great things happening in our lives, but also putting it out there if we have challenges, as well as using the platform as a networking tool to help us in our careers and home life. Circles of trust are part of it, because we may be experiencing similar hurdles, and have each other's backs. No judgement. Giving credit to one another and being happy for others is certainly a huge basis of Global Girls, and why women love being a part of it. It allows you to be happy for yourself but also allowing others to be happy for you too. This is magic. Additionally, when you have a voice and are a part of something, you feel more empowered and inspired to do greater things, not only for yourself but for others.

There is a new girls' club in town, as we haven't seen before, not just isolated to Global Girls but generally out there in society. We welcome with open arms anyone that wants to jump onboard, who is seeking only encouragement and inspiration to go out and do what is in their heart and mind. The *Global Girls* book will give you an insight to how we are all different, travelling in the same boat but through different sunshines and storms. But we all have one thing very much in common, and that is we want to create a supportive network, we want to be heard, and we want to listen and give a helping hand and voice when required.

On behalf of all the Global Girls, we thank our loving family, friends and supporters. Our world is a better place, because of you.

KAREN GEE

Entrepreneur | Wife | Mother
Passionate about helping women feel
their best.

Tell us your story to now

When I married and had the first of my five children in my early twenties, I had no idea of the journey my life would take. In fact, although knowing that I am a driven person, the following fifteen years were primarily focused on raising my family. It was in 2011, when my second son, Oscar, coaxed me into entering the Mrs Australia Globe pageant that my life began on a roller-coaster of epic proportions!

At the time I wasn't very confident. I'd lost my way and didn't know what I wanted for myself, so to say I was surprised when I was accepted with a letter saying they 'loved' my application, is quite the understatement! The next seven months were like a whirlwind, working alongside the other inspiring finalists, while raising funds and awareness for the two things closest to my heart – women and children.

The whole family came to watch me at the Mrs Australia Globe ceremony in Melbourne, and I was totally shocked when they announced me as the winner, and Mrs Australia Globe for 2012. Holding this prestigious title was very exciting, with amazing experiences and meeting influential people during that time. It sparked the drive and passion I'd always known was in me and I realised I wanted to find a way to empower women to be the best version of themselves. I wanted to encourage every woman to feel good about herself, regardless of shape and size, as every woman deserves to feel special.

At the time, I found myself sketching dresses, and then quickly hiding them in the drawer! It was my husband who encouraged me to take a leap of faith and go for it! With no formal fashion design or business training I took the leap into developing my business. I knew I wanted to create fashion that would help every woman feel beautiful, while flattering her uniqueness. I knew I wanted to create a sustainable brand and use ethically sourced fabric that would always look good and not crease. I had a lot of boxes to tick!

I was ready to launch my business in early 2013. I'd met some amazing contacts in my experience as Mrs Australia and a stylist I knew was dressing actress Demi Harman for the Logies. I was astounded when she chose my dress. From there, we've never looked back. The website crashed because we had so many enquiries. I have to admit, I probably wasn't ready for the snowball effect that happened after that, but I picked up the ball running and got through the roller-coaster that is business management and we opened our store in Chifley in 2015, along with our own manufacturing plant soon after.

Our dresses are now chosen by celebrities across the world, most notably Meghan, Duchess of Sussex. Although our dresses are our most famous look, we also customise tops, skirts, leather pants and evening dresses.

In 2017, I embarked on one of my biggest challenges so far; I attended Harvard in Boston, USA, and completed a prestigious business course. What an amazing experience!

It is now 2022, nine years since we launched Karen Gee and I'm surprised every day at how far we've come. The events of the last two years have been interesting, but I'm excited for the future. With the business well-established, I've been able to focus on the very values that brought me to where I am today – to encourage and empower women to be their best. Because I've been on the journey myself, I'm inspired to support women who have an entrepreneurial spirit and a dream they want to bring to realisation. If you can dream – you *can* do it!

What is your *why*?

As simple as it sounds, your *why* can be a very hard thing to define. It took me a long time in my life (in my thirties) to have that *aha* moment – when I knew I had found it, I felt fulfilled and at peace, because I had been searching for so long. Prior to finally discovering my *why,* I would always question myself as to how I was making a difference in not only other peoples' lives, but my own.

When I was young, I would work hard in my parents' businesses, learning the fundamentals to running a business, and the importance of connections and customer service. Whilst I enjoyed this part of the businesses, I didn't enjoy the business itself – I did it because it was what we did to put food on the table and survive.

In my twenties, I married and had five treasured children, which were my number one priority. To be present as a mother and wife was something that took most of my time. It only occurred to me much later, after I had children, that I was missing a vital ingredient to my drive and happiness, and that was finding my purpose – my *why*. The harder I tried to find it, the more distant it seemed to be. At one point, I never thought I would find it. Then one day, out of the blue, I received a call to say that I was chosen as a finalist for Mrs Australia Globe, an event that encourages women to step out of their comfort zone, to raise money for much-needed charities, and to engage with other women and businesses to create your personal brand.

Whilst I never once assumed I would win the competition, I embraced the opportunity to meet other people and connect with inspiring humans. Over a period of eight months, I threw myself into helping others and raising much-needed funds for the charity organisations. This gave me a lot of joy and the ability to use the experience and knowledge I had. One thing that I did lack was a lot of self-esteem – I felt intimidated by all others, so that was definitely out of my comfort zone, but something I overcame by ensuring I networked with as many people as I could.

Like a lot of women, I always saw the best in others, but never the best in myself. It was my goal to be more confident and self-assured. I went on to be the winner of Mrs Australia, and I knew that if I were to make a difference with the title, I would need to be a voice. I wanted to use the platform to inspire other women to be their best and focus on themselves before they influenced other people. I did this by becoming an advocate of positive body image.

Working with the Butterfly Foundation as the spokesperson, I did a lot of public speaking and presentations, and became the ambassador for brands that make a difference in other peoples' lives. I knew that after my reign of being Mrs Australia, I would continue my journey of networking and helping others. I wanted to bring together my love of fashion, yet ensure that I was making women feel beautiful and confident at the same time. So, Karen Gee was born. I wanted to create a brand that focused on women – all women, no matter their shape, size, colour or background. I wanted to present an opportunity to all women, and I started this journey by launching by Karen Gee with five basic black dresses. I had no idea how this would be received by the public, but I was willing to back myself, work hard and stick to my ethos. The response was incredible, with the brand growing faster than I could keep up with, which lead to launching a KG flagship store in Sydney and the purchase of a production house to manufacture the KG garments.

Your *why* and purpose are not the same things. Your passion/purpose is your mission in life, *why* is the reason you do the things you do. Look for things that make you feel excited, happy and content. Your *why* is like your signature, unique to you and what makes you so wonderful. Your *why* should never cause you anxiety, it should drive you to be inspired and motivated.

My *why* (my driver) is that I am fulfilled when I am giving back and enabling people to feel great about themselves, whether it is through the garments I produce, being consistently mindful of kindness to others, or doing random acts of kindness.

What is a challenge you have overcome?

The first real feeling of imposter syndrome I experienced was in 2017 when I attended Harvard Business School in Boston.

Whilst it was exciting to be accepted into this program, the excitement lasted about five minutes. My thoughts then turned to, *I am going to be amongst some of the most intelligent women in the world,* CEOs of big businesses, people that worked in the White House and billionaires, to name a few. I started to feel sick and questioned what I could possibly do to add value to these people. I will never forget the first day. I felt very alone, but at the same time, very brave. I walked into this huge class-room, anxiously looking around for my name tag – hoping that I would find it and it was not a joke that I was actually there. Name tags indicated your role and the company you worked for. As I glanced around, I could feel my heart pumping so hard – thinking, *I could run right now and no-one would ever know!* But instead, I silently slotted myself in behind the desk with my name, politely smiling at the attendees either side of me. The first case study lecturer arrived and we commenced. I am guessing that most of the women there had similar feelings on that first day, but by day three we had formed a wonderful routine and friendship and support of one another. In the end I realised that yes, these women were smart and working for some of the best companies in the world, but I was still able to add some value. I learnt from these amazing people about the detailed foundations of systems and processes which was something I didn't enjoy, therefore always avoided in my busi-ness. I have a new-found love of systems and processes, which is now instrumental in my businesses. Attending Harvard and overcoming imposter syndrome was one of the biggest chal-lenges I have accomplished. I didn't think I could ever do it but knew if I wanted to grow my brand, and me as a person, I had to take the leap of faith, go so far out of my comfort zone and just do it.

Whether it is Harvard, or just doing something you don't feel comfortable doing, my recommendation is to just do it, because it will give you more confidence to continue to try more.

What advice would you give women starting in business?

Generally, most women have a fear of failing and it is scary. Often our lives are dictated by what others think, and more often than not, it will make you question what you are doing. Although entitled to it, everyone has an opinion, however, if you feel what you are doing is right for you, and will benefit and enhance your life somehow, you must act. You are much better off acting and failing, than wondering *what if?* In most instances, if you have passion and purpose, chances are you will succeed in some form or another. The question you must ask yourself is, *What is the worst that could happen?*

For me, I wanted to create garments that made women feel beautiful and empowered. As simple as it sounds, it is no easy task when you don't even know how a garment is created. With no design training or experience in the fashion world, I took it upon myself to learn from the very beginning – Google was my best friend, and hustle was what got me to where I am today. The basis to all of this was that I had a purpose, I had a passion – and those two things enabled me to continually strive to find ways to bring this to life. It is no easy task, but if I can do it, anyone can. Every move forward and decision you make, must be aligned with what your purpose and passions are, step by step (may be one step forward and ten back to begin with), but you will get there, and you will look back and be so glad you did. You must be prepared to fall over many times, but instead of this being a roadblock, think of it as a way to become stronger and more resilient to get the results you want. Don't listen to others if they are negative, don't let others deviate your journey. I launched my brand in a time that fashion was totally saturated, most fashion labels had gone offshore and most creative ideas had been overused. I had to think in a way that allowed me to be unique in a large industry – my message consistent and my product of high quality. I always asked myself, *How do we do it differently? How do we appeal to our defined audience? How do I enable our message to be truly authentic?* So, I turned selling a garment into selling an experience – an experience where the customer goes on a journey with the brand, to ensure credibility and a sense of ownership for them. Too many times to remember, people would say it's not possible, which drove me to be more determined than ever to prove them wrong, but more so to prove to myself that I am capable and brave enough to keep pushing to bring all my ideas together and have a valuable offering to women all over the world. My top tips to others that are thinking of beginning a business, or starting a new career are:

1. Go with your gut – it is always right.
2. Don't listen to others if the feedback is negative.
3. Network, network, network – don't underestimate this.
4. Create credibility.
5. Always have a foundation of defined purpose for your business or career and align all decisions with this.
6. What inspires you to share your passion with others?
7. Let's not get passion confused with purpose. Passion is a

powerful or compelling emotion or feeling. Purpose is the reason for which something is done, created or for which something exists.

So, I have made my passion a reality, and I want to share it with as many people as possible. I am passionate about 'The Dress' because I get to share it with so many, without defining or categorising any shape, size, colour or background. I consistently witness the joy of women who choose Karen Gee, and I am rewarded with happiness.

My brand to me is both personal and professional, and I truly believe that is what sets the KG brand apart from anything else. How we make you feel is part of the journey at KG.

What do you want your style to say about who you are? Some say that what you wear shows your identity like your upbringing, your wealth, how smart you are and how influential you are. Whilst I respect this is the opinion of some, I don't agree, and think your style should come from your personality and what you feel most beautiful in. If we were judging my style and what it says about me, it depends when and what day you ask me. Weekends I usually wear training gear, shorts, and yes at times, thongs (the Queenslander in me), weekdays, it is usually a timeless, elegant KG dress, with sandshoes (nice ones) and little make-up, and on other days, I glam it right up. If I had to sum it up – I guess, unique.

ABOUT KAREN GEE

My name is Karen Gee, I am a wife, mother of five children (four boys and a girl), who will always be my babies, but have now grown into fine young people of society. Further, I am a huge advocate of supporting women – all women. It has long been a passion of mine, and I truly believe my purpose in life, to encourage and empower women all over the world to do what makes you most happy, and there is no wrong or right in what you choose, as long as you are happy. In 2013, I began my journey into bringing together my love of timeless fashion for every BODY, with focus on designing and creating garments to fit every shape, size, colour and background. To me, each and every woman has beautiful qualitites and unique talents, and I wanted to help women celebrate this by having a hand in making them feel beautiful and confident in what they were wearing. I have never been captivated by any of the glory of being in fashion, rather the immense feeling of joy I receive when I know I have empowered another woman. This is everything. I have dressed royalty, worldwide celebrities, high net worth women, housewives, corporate women, sports stars, prime ministers' wives, the premiers, TV stars – all of which are equal. At the end of the day, we all want to feel our best, we all want to be confident and happy, and if I can have a hand in allowing this, I am a success story.

DR VANESSA ATIENZA-HIPOLITO

Doctor | Wife | Mother | Triathlete
Dedicated to educating women to be in charge of their breast health.

Tell us your story to now

I am a wife, mother of two young kids, sister and daughter. I was born and raised in Manila and completed my studies in medicine and radiology training in the Philippines. Sixteen years ago, I travelled from my hometown with only 30 kg of luggage and a 7kg carry-on bag to start a new life in Perth, Western Australia. I had to borrow money from my sister for my airfare, visa application and other expenses. Ever since I was a child, I knew I wanted to become a doctor – a paediatrician. While studying medicine, I got interested in surgery and wanted to become a paediatric surgeon. I even did three months pre-residency training in surgery. However, despite my passion and interest in surgery, I did not find enjoyment in this specialty. I found myself burnt-out, always tired and had no time to read and study after long twenty-four to forty-eight-hour shifts. I even had two near-death experiences during my commute where my back tyre burst and I fell asleep on my way home.

The life-changing moment where I realised that surgery was

15

not for me was when I fell asleep whilst assisting a surgeon. It was just after 6 am and he was doing an abdominal surgery. I had just completed my twenty-four-hour shift with no sleep and had been very busy doing rounds all night. While I was using a retractor to open up the patient's abdomen, I fell asleep and my knees folded and hit the operating table. Fortunately, my hands were still steady. and the sound immediately woke me up and the operating theatre full of nurses and the anaesthetist went silent.

I then realised that I did not want to be a mediocre surgeon. I did not want to be a burnt-out doctor who had no time to read books and study. I didn't even have time for myself, family or friends. I had no work-life balance.

I felt lost and deflated. I was determined to be a specialist doctor but I had no idea what I wanted at the time except to be a surgeon.

One of my besties from medical school called me one day while I was wallowing in my sorrows. She told me that there was a radiology trainee position available at the hospital where she was training as an obstetrician. She was a first-year registrar at that time. I told her that I wasn't interested in radiology. However, since I didn't have a job and was becoming a burden to my family, I applied for the position. After one week of being a radiology trainee at The Medical City in Pasig City, Metro Manila, I fell in love. I found my niche. After four years of training, I discovered that I could sub-specialise in interventional radiology. So, I performed with and assisted my mentor who was one of two interventional radiologists in the Philippines at that time. None of my fellow senior or junior trainees wanted to assist or perform intervention. I enjoyed my radiology training because it was a multi-specialty field where you help diagnose other specialists. As a radiologist, your job is to be an expert from head to toe and know everything about imaging of the head and neck, ENT, neuroradiology, chest, abdomen, obstetrics and gynaecology, musculoskeletal, breast, urogenital, cardiothoracic and image-guided intervention.

I also enjoyed my radiology training because I was able to make time for my family and friends. I was able to make time to meet up with my besties from medical school. I remember them telling me during one of our coffee chats that I was 'meant to be a radiologist'.

I was so inspired that my four-year goal was then to complete my fellowship position in interventional vascular radiology overseas.

After my training at The Medical City, I worked as a general radiologist at different small imaging centres, driving all around Manila, Quezon City, Pasig, etc. all day, every day. It was a lifestyle that I did not enjoy much because it was not financially rewarding. I only did that for less than a year. Like any Filipino, I knew that my future was overseas which would enable me to help my family financially.

In 2005, I migrated to Australia where I completed my sub-specialty fellowship training in interventional and vascular radiology at Sir Charles Gairdner Hospital.

That same year, I met Glenn and we got engaged and married. It was a whirlwind romance indeed, but we both knew that we were mature individuals who were destined to be together.

Global Diagnostics, which is now Apex Radiology (Australia), gave me the opportunity to flourish as a junior radiologist. I was able to travel to remote areas like Bunbury, Kwinana, Mandurah, Esperance, Kalgoorlie and Northam. It sparked my interest in interventional procedures. I flew or drove to these sites to perform joint and spine procedures which I truly enjoyed.

In 2014, after completing my ten-year moratorium, I acquired ownership of Women's & Breast Imaging (WBI) together with my husband.

I lead the team as a business owner, clinical director and principal breast imaging specialist. I am committed to creating a positive, healthy, inclusive workplace environment for staff and patients.

I am also very passionate about educating general practitioners and women with regards to breast health. It is rewarding to talk to patients and see their happy tears when you tell them they have no breast cancer or when they say they appreciate the personalised breast care service we provided. It is heartwarming to talk to women after their breast cancer diagnosis and the gratefulness received for saving their lives.

Last year, I was appointed as an adjunct senior lecturer at Curtin University Medical and early this year (2021) at University of Western Australia Medical School. Since last year, I have been supervising medical students during their selective placements here at WBI. It is my goal to inspire them to hopefully consider choosing a career in specialist radiology.

I am thankful and grateful that I know my mission, I love what I do and I know I do it well. I love to teach and share my time and knowledge with the students.

Throughout my childhood, I attended Catholic schools and

was active in the religious community. When my mum and dad separated when I was nine years old, our faith and church community was our refuge. Our belief has kept us strong through all the obstacles we've encountered. While I was in medical school, I joined the students' choir group and played the organ accompaniment during masses.

Even now, in my busy life as a doctor with my own imaging centre, I always prioritise my service to God through choir. We sing in the church choir weekly, with my husband as our choir master and accompanist playing the keyboard or piano. Friday is my favourite day of the week because no matter how busy or tired I've been, choir allows me to belt out all the stress of the week. Then during Sunday mass service, I celebrate and give thanks to Him for all the blessings myself and my family have received.

I believe that my work is my destiny and I pray and thank the Lord for every milestone and blessing in my life, studies, work and family.

What is your *why*?

Like any kid living in a Third World country, my dream back then was to become a doctor so I could help cure people and provide for my mum financially. My dad left us when I was nine years old. My mum was the sole breadwinner in the family. She was working full-time, rode public transport to and from work, left home early and arrived late already tired with little time for me and my sister, who was only five years old. We were looked after by maids and only had time with my mum on weekends. I love my mum so much and I appreciated all the sacrifices she made to feed and educate us.

We used to live in a two-storey apartment next to my cousins. Every year during monsoon season, the first floor of our little home would be flooded up to knee- or even waist-height. All our furniture would be under the dirty floodwater which was usually mixed with canal water from the backyard drain. It was smelly. I always saw my mum and our maid using buckets to manually remove all the water once the flood subsided.

There were also some years where my mum didn't have a job but she would always pray and tell us that she was not worried because 'God will provide'.

My sister and I both finished university with the help of my dad – as per agreement with the lawyer that he would provide support for our school tuition until we graduated. I chose one of the expensive and exclusive private university schools. I was an average student, but I am proud that I completed my pre-medicine three-year trimester course on time. It was the only school in the Philippines with that program during my time and it was challenging. I was one of the students who graduated without failing a subject. Only one-third of us managed to do this.

After medical school and even after my radiology specialty training, income as a junior consultant radiologist was not enough. It was not sustainable. I could not afford to buy my own car and I couldn't afford to leave my mum and rent or buy on my own. My mum was still working full-time and helping me financially. I was determined to help her in return. I applied for fellowship positions all over the world, including Australia. I already knew that my future was not in the Philippines but overseas. I had a big dream and was determined to achieve this goal.

My plan was to study for one year and come back to Manila and practice what I learned overseas. I was so blessed that I was able to send money to my mum and nana every fortnight to support their daily needs including food allowance and household expenses.

However, the universe/God had other plans for me. In 2005, I arrived in Perth, met Glenn, got engaged and married him all in the same year.

In 2007, before I gave birth to my son, my mum was finally able to retire from her work and visit me here in Australia. She was happy to stay in Perth for a year to help me take care of my son, especially when I went back to work in a public hospital for additional training when he was only three months old.

Even though I was a certified radiologist in the Philippines, I had to undergo additional training. I ended up doing an additional five years of accredited fellowship training in different sub-specialties of radiology. Wow, four years in radiology in the Philippines and five years fellowship training in Australia!

I made many sacrifices whilst studying – working full-time, doing on-calls, working nights, weekends and public holidays, sometimes during Christmas and New Year. I even stayed late at work just to study to avoid distractions from my kids and on weekends, I usually went to the public library to study. I was so grateful for my mum and my in-laws who were always around to look after my young kids while I studied. I am also thankful and blessed that Glenn was very understanding and supportive.

As a doctor working in public hospitals and corporate imaging centres, you have a fixed full-time work week. In addition, you have the responsibility to work after-hours, weekends and public holidays. I missed significant events in my kids' lives.

As a business owner, my church and family are my priorities. I now have the privilege to take time off work to attend school assemblies, concerts, awards, sporting events, doctor's appointments and competitions, even during working hours. I enjoy being an 'Uber-mum' for my kids. I enjoy our bonding moments during our commute to and from school and after-school extracurricular activities. Going away on holidays is also easier compared to being a full-time employee.

I am enjoying being a loving wife and mum, and being a present mum is a blessing. I get to see them grow. I have a work-life balance where I can make time for ME TIME (exercise, enjoy OWS, running and triathlons) while still managing my own business, building an EMPIRE on top of being a specialist doctor, and I am saving lives and serving my local community via church choir service.

I am committed as an expert specialist in breast imaging and intervention to serve and care for the breast health care needs of women in my local community as well as the underserved and unmet needs in remote and regional Western Australia. Many women are still unaware of the enormous advancement in medical imaging technology in breast cancer detection and diagnosis. The standard of care for screening women over fifty has remained unchanged for twenty years. My patients are my inspiration, especially the breast cancer survivors.

It is my mission to educate women regarding the advanced technology available for early breast cancer detection and diagnosis, not only for women in the screening age group but also women younger than fifty years and older than seventy-five. Early detection saves women's lives and decreases breast cancer death rates.

WBI's mission is to provide a boutique personalised service to women by providing a one-stop-shop service which includes breast tomosynthesis, breast ultrasound, image-guided biopsy procedures and gynaecological ultrasound. I am hoping to raise awareness about breast cancer checks and preventive medicine as well as motivate women to prioritise self-care by making time for regular annual or biennial breast imaging tests.

Overall, I am just starting my journey. I am hoping to be an inspiration to all – women, students, immigrant university students and doctors, medical students, junior doctors, and fellow colleagues – who just need to light the fire that is burning inside them.

What is a challenge you have overcome?
Burnout
Whilst pregnant, I completed my training requirement for my college exam, studied late into the night, worked full-time as a fellow in paediatrics, breast and musculoskeletal, worked after-hours, did on-calls, weekend shifts and public holidays. When I had my eldest son, I took only three months off and started working again as a fellow at Princess Margaret Hospital (now relocated and named Perth Children's hospital). I was still breastfeeding. I would usually go to the doctors' quarters to express milk during my lunch break. It was challenging because I would have no time for a proper lunch. Sometimes, I would prefer to drive from PMH to East Perth where we used

to live just to feed him. Then I would go back to work. I was exhausted. In addition, it was depressing to see all the babies and kids at the hospital every day. Especially if the babies were the same age as my son.

I had my daughter the month of my college exam. I was so scared to go into labour during my MCQs. Due to emotional stress and exam pressure, I am embarrassed to admit that I consumed many pints of cookies and cream ice cream during the last trimester of pregnancy.

I was grateful and thankful that during these challenging times, I had my husband who was very supportive and a great dad to my kids. My mum and my in-laws were here in Perth for nine years taking turns to look after our kids whilst both of us were working.

It was like I was on autopilot. I woke up, worked, got home, tried to make time for my family but also had to study. Most of the time I would stay at work after office hours to study just to keep away from distractions from my newborn.

After having my firstborn, I was fortunate to be offered a short-term advanced trainee position at Princess Margaret Hospital. As a new mum, it was heartbreaking to meet sick kids and distressed parents. It gave me a lot of anxiety and sadness to see their sufferings and illness.

I was then offered a two-year training position in breast imaging at Sir Charles Gairdner Hospital and Royal Perth Hospital. Since then, I have met a lot of consultant radiologists who supported my preparation for the Royal Australian and New Zealand College of Radiologists (RANZCR).

After passing the college exam and being a qualified fellow

of RANZCR, another challenge was looking for a job. I didn't realise at the time, but according to the Australian Government Department of Health, as an immigrant doctor, we are all subjected to a ten-year moratorium which means we are only allowed to work in a district of workforce shortage. This meant that I could only work in remote areas until I completed my ten years here in Australia.

For three years, I dedicated my life to being a travelling breast radiologist. I committed to drive a four-hour return trip every other Friday to Bunbury which is 160 km from Perth. I usually left home at 5 am to be at SJOG Hospital Bunbury to attend the regular breast multidisciplinary team meeting at 7:30 am. Then I would start my full list of assessments of patients and biopsy procedures which took the whole day. Some days, my work would not be finished until after 5 pm. For three years, I drove home physically, mentally and emotionally exhausted. During winter, I left home in the dark and drove back home in the dark. Driving during the rainy season could also be dangerous. Most of the time, I would take two or three stops at petrol stations to rest. There are days that I could not remember how I got home because I was so tired.

I decided to resign – I couldn't risk my safety anymore. In addition, the traffic back home got so bad that the drive became three hours instead of two.

I made the huge decision to stop sacrificing my health and safety and resigned from the job that I thoroughly loved and enjoyed doing. I decided to be a present mum to my family. I also decided to focus on my WBI business full-time so I could give my undivided attention to my staff and clients.

MINDSET SHIFT – Mental game

I fell in love with triathlon when a student sonographer challenged me to race with her in a woman's triathlon event in 2017. I thought I could swim because I did swimming lessons one summer break when I was in high school. Little did I know that I could not even swim more than 10 m of the lane pool. I persevered and taught myself freestyle. I completed my first enticer triathlon race – I was so overwhelmed and I felt like I was dying during the ocean swim leg. It was my first time swimming in the ocean. I completed the 250 m ocean swim doing backstroke and I was the last person out of the water. The lifesaver kept asking me if I was okay and if I was ready to be pulled out of the water. I was determined to finish the race and get my first triathlon medal. I did finish my swim, bike and run, but not as the last person to finish the race.

Since then, I was hooked. I said to myself that I needed to work hard on my weakness. I invested in myself and enrolled into adult swimming lessons and stroke technique correction courses and workshops. I did more triathlon events but never managed to improve my swim. I never enjoyed swimming in the ocean or Swan River. I was always the last person out of the water – but never the last person in the race. I even had many traumatic experiences with the nasty stingers. I then found my swim coach, Dan, he taught me how to swim from the beginning. From basic front crawl technique. I was diligent in attending his swim lesson weekly for two years. Since then, I have completed many ocean water swim races including the iconic Busselton Jetty one-mile swim and OWS events here in Perth. I love meeting my swim friends at Coogee beach or Cottesloe to do our social swim then coffee catch-up. During summer, I love going to Cottesloe beach to do my after-work swim. Swimming helps me to switch off and not think about work. My favourite time to swim is before sunrise so I can watch the sun rise up over the horizon and see the beautiful sunrays reflecting on the ocean while doing my very early-morning swim. It is always MAGICAL! While 99% of the world's population is asleep, it feels good to enjoy my swim and be one with nature.

During the COVID-19 pandemic, I am proud of myself that I broke my personal record of swimming one to two miles, three times a week for the whole year of 2020. Even during lockdown, while the aquatic centres were closed, I kept swimming in the ocean. I am blessed that my work and residence are only five minutes away from the beach. Even during winter, I went out to swim with my friends and Dan with my wetsuit. I was able to achieve a total of over 80 km for 2020!

Servant leader and reinvention during COVID-19

As a health care provider, WBI was able to adapt, evolve and thrive during the COVID-19 pandemic. We remained open for half-days only for five weeks whilst in lockdown. Although we had low patient numbers, WBI was able to provide breast care health service to women in our community whilst BreastScreen WA and other private imaging providers were closed. In fact, WBI's breast cancer case numbers in 2020 were the same as previous years pre-COVID. It was fulfilling to provide optimal breast care service and save women's lives during the pandemic.

During the pandemic, I was binge-watching and totally immersing myself in personal growth books, audiobooks, webinars and online courses. It has given me an opportunity to PIVOT myself as a person and professionally as a doctor and business owner.

Challenges and obstacles in my life prepared me and moulded me to become the person that I am today.

The journey taught me how to manage my time and have WORK-LIFE BALANCE by knowing my priorities and non-negotiables.

What are your future plans?

Business

I am devoted to personal and professional growth and development to lead and guide a successful team with unique gifts and talents. I am also proud that I now lead a multicultural team of subspecialists and passionate professionals who are fulfilling our mission of providing 'caring commitment to women and our patients'. As a leader, I created a positive and supportive culture to help my team flourish and continuously mentor them to discover our team's *why* and *how*.

We are about to start our trial period on artificial intelligence using digital mammography in October 2021. I am investing in women's breast health by providing the latest technology in breast imaging and intervention. After forty-one years of WBI history, we are opening a new branch here in WA in 2023! I am starting to build my EMPIRE!

Academic

I am currently a co-author in two collaborative books including this one. I am also collecting my breast cases for future publications or digital courses.

I also submitted my first draft for The Brilliant Foundation article.

I enjoy my involvement with Curtin and University of Western Australia Medical School as a lecturer, mentor and supervisor. I enjoy supervising medical students during their pre-clinical selective placements at WBI.

Extracurricular and sports

My goal before I turn fifty years old is to be able to complete the iconic Busselton Jetty 3.6 km ocean swim, complete another ironman 70.3 race, complete another full marathon and port to pub 21 km ocean swim relay.

Hopefully before I turn sixty, my goal is to complete many 'run-cations' interstate and in different countries all over the world including in Europe, America and Asia.

What advice would you give women starting in business?

1. Learn to develop your growth mindset. Every person has the potential to be great and to achieve their dream job and goal. One should be persevering. You can achieve anything if you put your heart, mind and soul into it 101% of the time. To manage all aspects of one's life, aim to be 1% better each day by practising daily personal development. Practice self-care and self-compassion.

2. Sponge principle: Never stop learning. Soak up everything towards one's personal and professional development. Reading insightful books is a great way to invest in your personal growth. Honestly, I was able to pivot myself and my business when I fell in love with reading personal and

professional development books and audiobooks. I also attend a lot of webinars related to radiology and breast imaging and professional and personal development sessions on growth mindset. I attended a career advancement and leadership skills for women in health care online course last year. Add some purpose to your life with my ultimate favourite authors: Robin Sharma, Rhonda Byrne, Hal Elrod, Melinda Gates, Jeff Olson, Mel Robbins, Dale Carnegie, Adrian Gostick, Simon Sinek, Gabby Bernstein, James Clear, Brendon Burchard and Maggie Dent.

3. Find your *why*. Use it to fuel you towards your goals. Be open to adapt, evolve and transform towards any internal and external situation.

4. What God has predestined us for is the purpose He has given us. Looking back, I believe that God had faithfully weaved every situation in my life. He has given and surrounded me with earth angels to lead me to my destiny here in Australia – to find my dream job, meet my forever-love Glenn and be a gift and blessing to my family, friends, relatives and community. I am thankful and grateful that I am living for God's purpose.

5. Get fit and keep well mentally. Being physically fit provides clarity in my day. When the weather is good, I ride to work and back. It is an amazing start to the day to have a dose of endorphins. On weekends, I love to do long runs and ocean swims. In particular, running motivates me to be creative with my goals in life and at work. Keeping fit offers wellness and mental health.

6. Connect and give back to the community. As an immigrant

radiologist from the Philippines who arrived here in Perth to do further subspecialist studies and training sixteen years ago, I am blessed to call Australia my home. It is an honour and privilege to be able to give back and SERVE my community. I enjoy being a mentor and supervisor to junior doctors and medical students. I am proactive in giving back to my community by providing my pro bono medical and community health educational events regarding breast health and imaging updates. I am an advocate for the work of The Ladybird Foundation. I personally raised funds for the Foundation through my successful completion of the marathon in the 2016 City to Surf and my participation in the 2016 Tour de Gracetown bike ride. I am a proud supporter via personal fundraising and research of the following:

a. 100 Women Corporate Sponsor 2020: 100women.org.au

b. Breast Cancer Care WA: breastcancer.org.au

c. Breast Cancer Research Centre WA: bcrc-wa.com.au

d. DT38 Foundation Western Australia: ultrasoundservices. com.au/dt38-screening

e. Can 40 start 45

ABOUT DR VANESSA ATIENZA- HIPOLITO

Dr Vanessa Atienza-Hipolito MD FRANZCR is a specialist radiologist with subspecialty interests in breast imaging and intervention, musculoskeletal imaging, interventional and vascular radiology and paediatric radiology. She leads the team at Women's and Breast Imaging (WBI) in Cottesloe, Western Australia as a business owner and clinical director. WBI is a forty-one-year-old business which she took over in 2014. It is a boutique breast imaging centre based in a heritage listed building, the only private imaging centre in Western Australia which offers a one-stop-shop dedicated in screening and diagnosis of breast diseases in women, but also including paediatrics and men. This centre is a leading provider of the latest technology in mammography to improve early detection of cancer which includes (Volpara) advanced breast density measurement and digital breast tomosynthesis.

WBI services offer all imaging and image-guided biopsy modalities relating to the breast (except MRI): mammogram (3D-breast tomosynthesis), breast ultrasound, core biopsy, vacuum-assisted core biopsy and excision, fine needle aspiration biopsy (FNA), ultrasound guided abscess and cyst drainage, breast implant assessment and surveillance and gynaecological ultrasound.

In addition, she provides teleradiology reporting for Ultrasound Services which provides general ultrasound service for local and remote WA in Mandurah, Applecross, Harvey and Armadale.

Dr Vanessa is committed and passionate about clinical teaching and mentoring junior doctors and medical students. She is an adjunct clinical senior lecturer, clinical supervisor, OSCE examiner and clinician-student mentor at the Curtin Medical School, Curtin University, and adjunct clinical senior lecturer and clinical supervisor at University of Western Australia.

She worked for BreastScreen WA Bunbury Assessment Clinic as lead breast radiologist and as a screen-reader at BreastScreen WA East Perth head office from 2014 to March 2017.

Dr Vanessa was named AusMumpreneur 2021 in the following categories:

People's Choice Awards – Making a Difference (Local Community) Gold Award Winner

Health and Wellbeing Business Silver Award Winner

She was also named as finalist for the 2021 AusMumpreneur Awards in the following categories:

AusMumpreneur of the Year Award

Business Excellence Award

Women's Champion Award

In June 2019, Dr Vanessa was awarded the Millennial Achiever Award presented by Filipino Australian Club of Perth Inc (FACPI) during the Philippines Independence Day Gala Night at The Crown Towers, Perth, WA.

She is married with a son and daughter and contributes actively to her community in numerous ways by providing pro bono health education, ensuring they have access to current information on optimal care for breast health and the best available breast imaging technology. It is her passion to help women and raise awareness on the importance of breast checks and early breast cancer detection. She is an advocate of preventive medicine. As a founding member of The Brilliant Foundation, she has published two articles to share her knowledge and expertise, highlighting the importance of preventive medicine in breast health.

She is a great supporter of medical research through personal fundraising and carries out clinical research in her own field. She has presented in numerous local and international medical conferences. The highlight of her career was when she was invited to be a speaker and faculty in the 105th Scientific Assembly and Annual Meeting, Radiological Society of North America (RSNA) in Chicago USA in December 2019. The topic of her presentation was Breast Imaging in Western Australia: How we do it in the Land Down Under, A Case-based Review of the Breast (Interactive Session).

In her spare time, she loves singing in the choir, triathlon, swimming in the ocean, running, cycling, playing tennis, playing Scrabble with the family and travelling. The highlights of her travels were when she completed half-marathon races in Budapest, Hungary, and Bordeaux, France. She is eager to do more 'run-cations' in the future.

wbi.net.au

ANNA DARTNELL

Operations Executive | Mother | Wife
Passionate people leader & recovering perfectionist.

Tell us your story to now

I'm a woman, a wife, a mother and a friend. In the workplace, I'm an operational leader; someone who leads a big business and gets things done. I'm often described as a female leader – a title I embrace, having spent years growing my career in environments where women were either in the minority, or completely absent.

My story now is one of managing the often-competing roles carried by female leaders, and successfully doing so, thanks to the support of an extraordinary cheer squad and the experience gained over an unusual journey.

Today, I have the great privilege of being general manager a large operational business in Western Australia. It's a challenging executive role, which fills my days and continues to bring me great joy. I work with an extraordinary team, who provide supply chain and logistics services to mining and bulk commodities customers across Western Australia. We operate trains, trucks and terminals to move our customers' products from regional Australia and connect them with export markets across the globe.

As a female executive in the transport and logistics sector, I acknowledge I don't fit the traditional norm for a general manager. Although, having had a career which has encompassed industry experience in resources, manufacturing, road, port and rail transport and professional services, I'm no stranger to being 'different' to those who've come before me. I'm quite proud to have built my career in what would be considered 'non-traditional' industries. Whilst it wasn't a conscious goal to choose a more challenging path, I'm pleased to have become a successful female role model and business leader and to have developed great relationships and support networks with awesome men and women through that journey.

My career path has been decidedly non-linear – more like a jungle gym than a ladder! I'm frequently asked, 'How did you get here?' and it's somewhat of a rambling answer, but in telling it, I reflect on the building blocks that underpin who I am and how I choose to use the skills I've been blessed with.

My journey started in a fairly unremarkable way. I was the youngest child of an engineer from Broken Hill, who found his niche in the mining industry in Western Australia, and a teacher, who followed him from one dusty north-west town to another throughout my early childhood. I attended school in Perth and went on to study industrial relations at the University of Western Australia, getting my first job in the WA mining industry.

Having commenced my working life in the world of human resources and industrial relations, my transition into operations management was a huge jump, at a time when I had no intention of making a change. I'd been working on a people project when

I was approached by the head of operations, with a proposal to move into the distribution centre, and ultimately to become his successor. The opportunity could not have been further from the direction I thought I was heading in. Furthermore, I had no experience in logistics. My first reaction was to burst out laughing and tell him he was crazy! Thankfully, my boss knew me well. He observed, 'I think you want to be the person making the decisions, not the person advising the decision-maker. Well, here's your chance.' I stopped laughing, took a chance on a complete career change and have never looked back.

Suddenly the onus was on me to engage, motivate and develop a large workforce; actually walk the talk I'd be advising others on for many years, and to do it in an environment in which women traditionally did not hold senior roles. I revelled in that change, genuinely thriving on the 'other side of the fence'. And whilst I had moved into supply chain with little more product storage expertise than that required to stock my own pantry, my background in the people space served to make me an infinitely more self-sufficient leader.

My early operations roles were strongly focused on business improvement, meaning I was able to draw on my existing change management skills whilst learning the principles of supply chain management. I quickly discovered that all the logistics knowledge in the world was meaningless if you weren't able to capture the hearts and minds of your people. So, whilst I've become recognised and respected for my expertise in logistics and supply chain, my strong foundations in workforce engagement and ultimately interpersonal connection have really been the keys to my success.

The move into operations had many twists and turns. It has involved sweat and tears, as well as plenty of joy and laughter. And with the addition of children into my life, it required some sacrifice and compromise, because I struggled to reconcile how to be the kind of mother I wanted to be and the kind of leader I needed to be, when I was running twenty-four seven operations both at work and at home.

But as we learn through experiences, our careers are seldom as brittle as we assume them to be. After a period away from leading large teams, the desire to return to it never left me. So, with my children a little older, I made a choice on where I wanted to focus time and grow my career. And I knew it was to become the strong female leader that I looked up to across my career journey. It was to step up and declare I wanted to lead an operation of my own and that I was capable to do so.

That's my story now. That's why I do what I do today. That's why, when people observe me at work, while they (like my family) might acknowledge the more-than-occasional long hours, they mostly notice the time I spend meeting with and talking to my team, sharing ideas and laughing as we embrace new challenges together. I have the best job in the world because I have a great team, a growing business and the ability to find the fun in all the challenges that combination brings with it.

And I know there are people, both men and women, who observe the way I go about the business of leading and see a different approach, a different energy and a different style to what might have been expected. And you know what, if that's the one thing I achieve in my world right now, that observation, that spark, that sense of enlightenment about what leadership looks like, it might just be enough.

What is your *why*?

My *why* is all about connection, and it's through connection that I feel the power to make a difference. It has taken me a while to recognise this central theme in my life, but connection underpins all the values and behaviours I hold dear. Creating a genuine connection with people, unlocking opportunity, sparking inspiration and finding the common purpose to bring people together really is the foundation of my working life and it mirrors my life at home and in my community – basically anywhere you see me apply discretionary effort.

I deeply believe that nearly everyone is looking for connection from each of the areas in which they invest their time. This drive to create connection is intimately linked with my drive to make a difference and I see this manifested in the four value statements I consistently return to throughout my days.

1. **If something needs doing, do it.** I believe we all have the capacity to make a difference but also recognise that only a few people are comfortable to push themselves to affect change. I'm easily frustrated by inactivity and struggle to sit back and watch, when observing a situation where there is a clear problem or a loss of momentum. When I see a need, a situation in which a relatively small act could build positive momentum, I'll challenge myself to get involved and equally, will challenge others to lean in and be that change they want to see. It's a challenge that tends to see me inject myself into situations and help others to see that their actions have the power to affect change.

2. **Work should be fun**. As with my life, my experience of work is strongly linked to the people I interact with and I believe we all work better with people we enjoy being around – be they colleagues, bosses, team members or customers. My career experiences, both the highs and the lows, have served to reinforce the value of investing in relationships, finding the fun and experiencing the joy in work. It's also helped me opt out of work environments in which I've been unable to sustain a sense of connection and fun (those awful transactional environments where you pour your energy into a situation that fails to feed your soul in return).

3. **You get out what you put in.** In my experience, results most frequently correlate to the effort expended. I value knowing that my contributions make a real difference within my family, my organisation and my community. I've experienced this positive impact to the same extent in our business, as I have done in our school P&C arts organisations, not-for-profit boards and in my friendship circles. Seeing and feeling the return on personal investment is my key to maintaining the energy and drive needed to succeed, especially when I encounter obstacles and inevitable frustrations.

4. **We have abundant capacity for the things that matter to us**. So, this one can sometimes be my undoing, because when you believe in abundant capacity, you tend to view life and your energy level as being a cup that will never run dry – and it's fair to say that I can occasionally run myself ragged with my 'it's only a little extra thing' mentality. However, I truly believe that we do make time for the things that matter to us – and when people say, 'I haven't had time to do that,'

what they are often saying, is that it's simply not something they want to prioritise. People frequently ask me how I have the time for all the things I'm involved in and my answer is always the same: these are all little things, and they're little things that mean something to me or things that rely on me to help someone else achieve meaning. When you believe in something strongly enough, when it truly is demonstrative of your values, you can make the space to excel – you simply need to be willing to look for the little ways in which you can help.

What is a challenge you have overcome?

Many of our perceptions of ourselves are formed in our school days, and success in youth is often intrinsically linked to achievement in school. As a student, academic achievement did not come easily to me and I became used to feeling I was not the smartest person in the room. Whilst this often resulted in disappointment, it also taught me from a very young age that I would need to work hard to be successful. The work ethic that instilled in me has become one of my most enduring habits and has been key to my success in every role I have undertaken. The challenge this has created though, is an expectation that I must work more, get through more, just *be* more, to really prove my worth.

Imagine the challenge that mindset creates when faced with impending motherhood and the inevitable juggle between what you want to do and what you're genuinely able to get done.

I'd always known and planned for children in my future. I had a great upbringing, with two married parents who are still together today after more than fifty years of marriage. I too found the love of my life in Roger and the addition of kids to our lives felt inevitable. That said, when it was actually upon us, and I was faced with the prospect of leaving a job I loved to take maternity leave, I found myself really challenged. I wanted to be a hands-on mum, I wanted to take the time to be home with my infant child, but I didn't want to miss anything at work. My career was going gangbusters at the time, so it felt bittersweet to have to put the brakes on. That said, I could see that with a twenty-four seven operational role at work and a twenty-four seven human being who needed me at home, something would have to give.

Clearly, I've always been ambitious and passionate about my work, and have found great personal meaning in achieving career success. Making adjustments to accommodate the arrival of this new little person in my life meant I needed to reconsider my expectations for career fulfilment in the short term. Becoming a mother and giving up what had been my dream role at the time, were huge obstacles for me to overcome. The fear of what my career would become after having children and the challenge of balancing my desire to be a great mother with my desire to maintain my professional self, were significant conflicts. The whole situation was made even more challenging when we moved interstate for my husband's career whilst I was on maternity leave. There was no going back to my old role, and I was left facing the unknown of a new marketplace and the need to find an opportunity that allowed me to contribute within the boundaries of a flexible work arrangement. It all seemed hugely daunting, and I was acutely aware that my historical bias towards 'just working harder than anyone else' wouldn't be on the table.

What it unlocked was the learning that I was more than the hours I could work and the tasks I could consume.

Feeling I had little else to rely on, I focused on my ability to take calculated risks when opportunities presented themselves and on my relationship-building skills. I 'hung a shingle' and chose to create my own opportunity as a management consultant. Project by project and contact by contact, my business grew organically. I built the business around my capacity to work, as many days and hours as I could commit without losing out at home. The focus was delivering the outcome required by the client rather than the hours in the office to do it. I'd found a match for both my life needs and my passion for work.

And while it provided a somewhat meandering route, it was that pathway which kept me active and eventually led me back into operational leadership. When I needed to step away after the birth of my daughter, I thought I would never go back. But what I learned is that life is a marathon and not a sprint – and one should never say never.

What are your future plans?

On any given day I find myself conflicted by this question.

For a long time, I was striving to be the best leader I could be. I wanted to prove myself by getting into progressively more senior roles and leading a large operational business. Through hard work and good fortune, I've been blessed to successfully deliver in that role today.

My natural drive to explore what's next continues to see me strive to achieve the highest role I can, which is likely to be leading a large, listed business. It weighs on me quite heavily that I am one of only a relatively small number of women running large transport businesses. Continuing to progress my career, be a role model to others and be a visible representation of a different style, background and look of leader in operations, does feel like an important part of my considerations on what's next.

That said, for all this ambition and drive to be a good role model, I often dream about running away with my family, living for an extended period in a tiny town in rural Italy and assuming a simple, more relaxed life. Perhaps my window for living *la dolce vita* in Italy closed for a while when my kids started high school, but the daydreams continue, and I suspect some form of extended getaway sits somewhere in our future.

Beyond these musings, I look to my future as being one that builds on the theme of connection and harnesses my network to empower others. I love sharing stories. One of my most favourite things is listening to people's stories, taking time to talk about the highs and lows of a life's journey – where they've come from, how they've overcome challenges along the way. I've found this bias towards sharing stories has been incredibly powerful when looking at the experiences of women at work. Working women are far from a homogenous group but I've seen a number of women face and overcome the challenges of being a first, or feeling like a token or a tiny minority within the male-dominated workplaces that have been central to my career. As I've moved into progressively more senior roles, I've consciously made time to talk about all the great and not-so-great aspects of my career. The building blocks to my success and the power of connection throughout my journey – the need for a cheer squad, a shoulder to cry on, a leader to really challenge you. All these stories have been captured and shared with the hope of capturing the imagination of others, harnessing a real-life example, because we're so often told that 'you can't be what you can't see'. I've been so fortunate to have built an amazing support network through my career and to have maintained my connections over time. I've never had to look far to find inspiration or advice. And at the risk of sounding dreadfully arrogant, I find great joy in the prospect of being that inspiration and giver of advice to others. Whatever direction my future journey takes me, I know I have reached a point where I have the privilege of a platform from which I can support others. And through quiet moments, as well as speeches made from podiums, I will be sharing stories that play their role in creating a world where women see themselves in every possible role and at every level within our society.

What advice would you give your thirteen-year-old self?
I have so many pieces of advice, much of which I try out on my now thirteen-year-old, who I marvel at in their completeness. I felt so very incomplete at thirteen and I wish I could go back in time and be able to provide some assurance that so much of what you worry about and allow to consume your thoughts, really doesn't matter.

My advice is to be free to meander. To embrace and share the joy in all the little things that make you laugh and connect with your friends. Enjoy the little moments where you can be without a care, silly and fun-loving, because they will undoubtedly be the memories that, thirty years later, you will still recall and will still bring a smile to your face.

Become comfortable sharing and expressing how you feel. You'll get there eventually but it'll take a while and if we start trying to connect with that space and express emotions now, rather than feel they are something to hide away, it will create the opportunity for so many more moments of joy instead of fear.

Wear tiny bikinis – your body is AMAZING and it's going to take you years to realise that – just trust me that it's awesome and you really *can wear that!*

You are amazing and you will achieve amazing things.

But more than anything, you are most definitely ENOUGH.

ABOUT ANNA DARTNELL

I'm a Anna Dartnell, a business leader who lives in a beautiful, riverside corner of Perth, Western Australia.

At home I'm mum to two teenagers, who grew up with two working parents and don't appear too damaged from the experience. Outside of my home, I'm a transport executive with broad experience, developed in a range of non-traditional roles, across a portfolio of iconic Australian businesses.

I began my working life in the Western Australian mining sector, fresh out of university with an arts degree – certainly not the normal background for a mining grad. After developing my early career in industrial relations and human resources, I moved across the country and into the manufacturing sector, where I was tempted into an operational management role, supervising a large warehouse operation. Over time, I developed industry-leading expertise in supply chain management, stepping into progressively more senior operational leadership roles.

I've loved my career in operations but my journey hasn't been a linear pathway. The fact I've made my unconventional career a success leaves me incredibly proud – I know I've succeeded in roles and environments in which women have historically been absent. This determination to carve my own pathway has been a source of influence and inspiration with others. I've demonstrated, through the tapestry of my career development, the joy to be found in operational careers. And I've used that experience to inspire others, specifically seeking to amplify the opportunities for women in non-traditional roles and industries.

I'm a high-energy people-person, and experience has shown that I'm skilled at engaging people and harnessing that engagement to drive outcomes. This approach has worked for me in the businesses I have led – and it's been an approach I've also taken to building female participation in operational roles and industries. As my career has progressed, I've actively sought to expand my reach and seek ways to both highlight and ignite opportunities for women in operations.

I believe that personal actions can make a big difference in our world and strive to be someone who takes action and doesn't wait for it. My passion for gender equality is about creating an inclusive world – one in which my daughter and son can each dream big and carve a path to achieve those dreams.

We have abundant capacity for the things that matter to us. When you believe in something strongly enough, when it truly is demonstrative of your values, you can make the space to excel in business, to nurture your family and connect within your community. The joy of this approach is that I love the sense of shared purpose and community connection that active involvement feeds.

As a business leader, I'm fortunate to have been recognised as a Telstra Business Women's Awards Finalist and a WA Business News 40Under40 Awards winner. However, at my core, I am a wife, a mother and a friend, who believes that we have abundant capacity when we put our energy into our passions.

MONIQUE ANDERSON

CEO | Wife | Mother | Coach

Passionate about helping others achieve their full potential personally and professionally.

Tell us your story to now

Where do I start on the story of Monique? I have certainly had a very colourful life. I was raised in hotels most of my childhood growing up in the Sydney CBD. Well, let's just say, watching *Underbelly* makes me laugh because that stuff happened, it actually happened! I matured quite early watching a lot of this and just observing people in general as we always lived on the premises. I knew from an early age that I had to get out into the world – I really didn't like school that much – I knew if I wanted to achieve anything I just had to go. I left school in year eleven and started out my career in the travel industry back in the good old days when every day included a long lunch at the Wentworth Hotel. This allowed me to travel overseas and live in America for a few years which I truly loved. Still not knowing really what I wanted, I decided hospitality was going to be my in-between job until I worked it out. I worked hard – I should have known that the work ethic I got from my mum was going to always take me to the top – and by the age of twenty-two I was the youngest female licensee in New South Wales, and it didn't stop there.

After having kids in the nineties, I moved to the Central Coast and ended up being the managing director of Central Coast Stadium. I can't remember how many female stadium managers there were in New South Wales or Australia at the time, but I know it was it was only a few.

It was at the stadium where I first met John Singleton. I started working for John back in 2000 and ended up CEO for the group. I worked for John for twenty years up until last year when my current husband and I started our own company. We achieved so many amazing things in that twenty years, we helped grow the Central Coast, securing much-needed funding through our federal campaign. We unsuccessfully tried to get the Coast its own NRL license – that experience ended up being more political than running for a federal seat! I represented John on numerous boards including the publicly listed Macquarie Radio which was an eye-opener and I thoroughly enjoyed as it allowed me to grow and see the other side of business. I was so lucky to have all these opportunities.

I guess you could say eight years ago my life changed. I had been separated from my husband for twelve months after being married for eighteen years. I was actually thinking about moving overseas but then I met my current husband, Paul. If someone had told me that I was going to be this much in love I would have told them they were insane as I didn't deserve to be happy. I used to dream about having the romances you see in the movies, the happy-ever-after moments that every girl imagines.

I had my *Twilight* moment, Paul ended up being my Edward,

he taught me how to love unconditionally and believe in myself. We live together, work together – we do everything together and that's how we love it, I don't think we could ever live apart. This is how it's supposed to be, this is how it's supposed to feel. But there was still something missing inside me.

What is your *why*?

I guess you could say Paul, my beautiful children and my family are my driving force but there is a new love that has surfaced and that is my personal development. I never would have thought I would include personal development alongside such treasures in my life, but it has completed me.

Even when I had everything I wanted, I used to have those stupid role play talks in my brain. I was the queen of questioning, being jealous, hating myself, constantly thinking about negative things that I had no control over, wishing bad things into our life instead of thinking about the positive things, thinking about things we really want that are really important to us. I swear when I look back at the things I used to put in my head it was just ridiculous.

However, I was also very good at laughing and putting on a confident, happy face to everyone else. Although, inside, I really didn't feel worthy or important, I knew I could hold my own in the boardroom, with ministers, prime ministers, politicians, CEOs, Australian icons or really anyone – it didn't worry me who they were or what they did, I knew I could achieve anything, and I am well respected with my peers. As soon as I was away from the work environment what I saw in the mirror was very different, and surprisingly, no-one else could see this. I was quite forceful, strong and powerful to everyone else but that's not what I saw inside. I didn't ever think that would change, I just thought that was how I was and would always be.

What is a challenge you have overcome?

When it comes to challenges, I've had quite a few and all of them have really come from the six inches between my ears. My self-confidence, my belief in myself and the guilt I had having to work full-time while raising my two treasured boys.

Let's start with my self-confidence. I never saw what other others saw in me – if I ever got a compliment, I would brush it away because I didn't believe them. I was forever looking at other people and just thinking to myself how beautiful they were and if only I could look like them, and I really just kept telling myself that I was not good enough. I spent all my time doing everything for everyone else and didn't do anything for myself. My kids played such an important part in my life, every spare second of the day that I had was spent making sure they didn't miss out on anything. I used to get told that I spoilt them, but I suppose I was overcompensating for working and they were my everything. I guess you could say that was the detriment of my first marriage. It takes two to work in a marriage and I can honestly say, looking back now, I think I spent more time trying with the kids than I did with my husband. I also allowed my passion for work and my work ethic to really control my life. Besides my kids, I gave my job whatever I had left, twenty-four hours a day, seven days a week, 365 days a year – I always made myself available. I guess that's how I was able to get to the top and stay there. It wasn't until my eldest son reminded me that every Christmas, birthday, holiday, really any weekend was always interrupted by work that I realised. That's pretty hard for a mum to hear. My two beautiful step-kids also had to live with us and our interruptions for the past eight years so it affected all our family, but I now know that I did the best job I could and my relationship with all my kids is amazing. I now have four gorgeous children, two beautiful daughters-in-law and two treasured grandsons; they are all amazing.

So, I guess all my demons I've mentioned above, the guilt and the lack of self-confidence kind of led me to where I am now. I really didn't know what I wanted to do, all I knew is that I had to change my priorities to change the way I felt about myself and my whole mindset. I remember hearing someone comment on the book *Feel The Fear And Do It Anyway* by Susan Jeffers. I really was not a big reader, but I thought, *What the hell?* Wow, this book certainly kickstarted me and lead me on the most amazing path of self-discovery that I really thought I could never ever achieve.

They say things happen for a reason. At the time of all this happening, my beautiful mother, who I treasure and adore, was diagnosed with a level four glioblastoma brain tumour. She was so amazing, fit, young and beautiful. It was just so sudden I knew that I had to change things and I wanted to spend more time with her. I knew I needed something to help me get through what was going to be such a difficult, heartbreaking time. I'm so lucky that I got to spend so much quality time together before we lost her later that year.

I found something that has always been inside me and that is my passion to help others. I found personal development in a way that I have not experienced before. I've done so many courses and different mindfulness sessions over the years, but I really needed something special to get me through that difficult time and it's still hard, my heart breaks every day, but I know how proud she would be of me.

Breaking away from corporate life, becoming a mentor and business coach I now know I found my forever job alongside running our own business with my amazing husband. Helping others has always been at my core and being able to build a team of like-minded people is so rewarding.

What advice would you give women starting in business?

One piece of advice I have for women starting out in business is don't be hard on yourself. Give yourself a break. Your children will be okay, you will be okay, just don't guilt yourself about having to work, don't guilt yourself about occasionally not being there. I used to carry so much guilt that's all gone now. I have no guilt because I did the best job I could, I just wish I had been able to tell myself that rather than put myself through so much agony.

The six inches between our ears can be our greatest ally and our worst enemy. We spend so much time looking at how we treat our physical bodies – creams, make-up, healthy food – if only I had invested a little bit more time in putting some goodness into those six inches, like they say goodness in equals goodness out. Even ten minutes a day reading a book, listening to a podcast, watching something online – as long as it's something positive to put in your head and your heart, it makes such a difference.

Things have changed now from when I first started out, so many things that I went through are just not acceptable now but, hey, we just dealt with it because that's what we had to do. Young women today have so much support, it's so good to see but there's still a long way to go. The mental, sometimes physical, innuendos and abuse that so many of us had to deal with in the workplace just shouldn't be able to happen. I was always strong enough to not allow it to affect me, it was just like water off a duck's back, but it should never have happened, and I suppose I should never have allowed it to happen, but I guess we were all so scared about losing our jobs, and as I was always in an industry that was male dominated, I was worried about looking weak amongst my peers. So, my advice to women, and really all people, is don't carry guilt, don't allow others to treat you badly, and love yourself, be proud of what you do and you can achieve anything. Be the best person you can be and you will succeed.

One final bit of advice is gratitude – never lose sight of what you have in your life now and what amazing things are yet to come.

ABOUT MONIQUE ANDERSON

Hi, my name is Monique Anderson and I was born and raised in the heart of Sydney. My parents owned hotels, so I guess living and growing up in that industry gave me a great insight into human behaviour and also shaped the direction I was going to end up in. I left school in year eleven, I knew it wasn't for me and I was just dying to get out into the world and show everyone what I could achieve. My first job was in the travel industry which was great fun back in the day (1986) – long lunches, lots of overseas trips – but sitting behind a desk was not going to be for me.

I decided to pack up at the age of nineteen and head off to conquer the world. I flew out by myself and headed straight to the USA. My first night ended up in a bar in downtown Washington DC, where I swear the stereotype pimp with a feather in his cap offered me a job. Now, if I hadn't grown up in pubs, I could have thought what a lovely man for being so nice, but having spent my childhood observing people, it kind of made me realise that I could survive and look after myself anywhere and through anything. I probably could have just stayed in America, but my pop got sick and I decided to move back home.

I think it was the right time for me to come back to Australia. I decided to just follow in my family's footsteps and give the hospitality industry a go. I worked hard, back-to-back shifts, even if it meant coming into work straight from a night out. In two short years I had worked my way from barmaid to the youngest female licensee in NSW.

It was at this job that I met my first husband, who is the father of my two sons.

In 1999 I received a call that changed my life forever. I was asked to run the new stadium at Gosford. The stadium was just about to open and they really needed someone to build a solid team and turn this venue into something amazing.

There weren't many female stadium managers at that time and being able to achieve what I did was amazing. However, I still wanted to go higher, and I ended up being elected to the board of the venue managers' association, which was another highlight of my career.

In February 2020, my life once again took a major change. My beautiful mother who had already survived breast cancer was diagnosed with a level four glioblastoma brain tumour. Although we had a wonderful surgeon who rushed her straight in and removed it, it was too late – new tumours were appearing and we eventually lost her in December last year. It was during this time, along with the COVID-19 pandemic, that I took stock on what was important in my life. It was the hardest thing I have ever lived through and my heart aches every day.

I turned to personal development books and courses and am now in the best place I have ever been. Although the pain is still there with my mum, I am a much better person, I have time for my family and also for myself. I have been able to work through all the guilt I had from thinking I wasn't there for the kids, all the self-doubt I had internally. My self-esteem inside was appalling – although I came across as a powerful businesswoman, I was a basket case inside. When I looked in the mirror, I hated what I saw, I bluffed my way through my whole life until now. But now when I look in the mirror I see that I am a confident, successful, kind and loving person in my own right. I finally have my North Star to lead me into the next stage of my life.

CARRIE ROGERS

Property lawyer | Wife-to-be | Mother
Adventure seeker & loyal supporter.

Tell us your story to now

I feel very blessed to currently have three life roles that give me enormous satisfaction, joy, pride, drive and fulfilment.

I am a partner at one of Australia's top tier law firms.

I am a mum to two beautiful girls.

And I am a partner to a loving, supportive fiance, who I joke must be one of the most patient people in the world to put up with me, but in all seriousness, is one of the most kind-hearted and patient people there is. I think we make a pretty good team – in all honesty, we balance each other out.

I am also a daughter, a sister, a friend and a colleague.

I cherish each role and look forward to what is still to come.

I have a younger brother and two amazing parents who are two of the hardest working humans I know. I grew up on acreage in East Kurrajong which, to give the location some context, is at the bottom of the Blue Mountains, out near Richmond and Windsor. As a kid I used to think there was nothing to do – I was wrong. We had dogs, horses, chickens, goats, rode BMXs, dirt bikes, went waterskiing down on the river and learnt how to drive a manual before the age of sixteen because that is just what you did.

Living now in the inner city, I love getting back out there and visiting my parents and brother, sister-in-law and nephew. I love the peacefulness of it all, standing on my parents' back verandah and staring down into the bush in the gully. I now also appreciate how much fun kids can have out there – possibly a very nerve-wracking time for parents, but you learn some amazing things and there is always an adventure to be had.

I remember when my parents moved house, at the time I was living in an apartment in the city and had gone out to help them get settled in. Dad and I were at the front fence trying to work something out with the automatic gate, it was scorching hot and we both just had shorts and thongs on. I noticed the dog was acting a bit strange and then realised it was because there was a snake coming across the road right towards us. I jumped – what you are not meant to do, of course – and then as I landed and froze, the snake went straight over the top of my feet (my bare feet) towards a tree. At this point, the snake, being a baby brown snake, turned to try and attack the dog. Dad reacted by grabbing the dog and pushing her out of the way and promptly told me to go and get Mum and for her to bring up a shovel. So off I ran, sending Mum up with the shovel whilst the dog and I went inside and watched from the safety of solid brick walls. Looking out the window, I could then hear Dad telling Mum what had happened which included, 'You should have seen how high she jumped!' whilst having a good chuckle. Unfortunately, the snake and I were just in each other's way. That night, back in my apartment in the city, I must admit that when the fan blew something, causing a shadow to flit across the floor in the apartment, I did jump (again).

I went to the local primary school and the local high school, and even though public speaking terrified me, I was the school captain both in year six and in year twelve. I was a good student, definitely a better student than athlete, but I still played tennis, was in the swimming squad and did multiple forms of dance as well as playing both the piano and later the drums. Towards the end of high school, I worked at a local optometrist and then also at one of the local hardware stores. I went straight to university after finishing high school and started working at a local suburban law firm and accountant office as well as continuing to work at the hardware store. I feel as though this mixed workload, together with my studies, put me in a great place when it came to managing conflicting client deadlines and demands, and remaining calm under pressure. It continues to help me to this day with the day-to-day juggle of life. I remember when I was at school, contemplating what I would do when I finished, my parents said I could do anything I wanted, although Dad did say that he would really like it if it was something that put my brains to good use. My mum was the first person that went to university in her family, and I was then the second. My parents encouraged both my brother and I to follow our dreams – whatever that may have been.

Towards the end of university, I tried to secure one of the coveted legal jobs as a summer clerk/graduate. I must say, I was pretty naive as to what law firms were looking for back then, and nerves did not make me a very eloquent interview candidate. I definitely let nerves get the better of me. I'm also not great at selling myself – even now, it is still something that I really need to focus on, it continues to feel foreign. During this time, I was still working at the small suburban law firm, which in hindsight, was both a baptism of fire and a blessing. I was really thrown in the deep end but the responsibility I was given and what I learned was invaluable. It provided such a great base for the lawyer that I have now become. I can't even remember exactly but I must have still been looking for opportunities to follow my dream of experiencing life in a big city law firm. I actually applied for a legal secretary/paralegal position at the firm I am still to this day currently at. Having worked in a small firm throughout most of my university years, where you get to do a bit of everything, from criminal matters to civil litigation to transactional work, I was adamant at that time that I wanted to either be a criminal lawyer or a transactional property lawyer. Having then gained experience in the city law firm, it became evident to me that I was better suited to transactional work. That partner that took a chance on me all those years ago became my mentor and champion in the partnership path and is now a dear, dear friend who I still regularly confide in and seek guidance from.

Even though I am still at the same firm, I did take a bit of a hiatus and go in-house which was fantastic. I love the whiteboarding (that's showing my age, isn't it) strategy sessions and working with the commercial team to pull all of the different parts of the deal together. During this time, I also had the opportunity to travel overseas on incredibly short notice with some great people to negotiate and see whether there were any new opportunities that we might look to secure. I thought I had a pretty good idea what I was getting myself into having worked for the client for many years but that was definitely not the case, I don't think you can truly appreciate what your client is dealing with unless you have experienced what it is like from the inside. After twelve months, and where I was at that time in my life, I decided that I wasn't quite ready to let go of the dream to try and become a partner at a top tier law firm. My time in-house was another invaluable opportunity and I strongly recommend it to junior lawyers, should the opportunity arise and to take that opportunity with both hands – it builds both your soft skills and technical skills.

I feel as though the dream to make partner was mostly to prove to myself that I could do it, and I did, at the age of thirty-three. I love what I do (most days) – I love getting into the trenches with the client and the team and strategising a deal, getting all of the pieces to fit together and then working as an extension of the client and being part of the team to see the deal reach completion or watching the development proceed through construction to practical completion and seeing the space activated, all the while knowing how the bits and pieces fit together.

It has been a crazy and fulfilling sixteen years on the work front and I would have to say the same on the personal side as well – I have made some amazing friendships including all of the women who are contributing to this book, I have become more resilient, I have worked on some amazing deals with amazing clients and colleagues, I helped build a granny flat from the ground up with my parents for my grandparents, I got a bike licence and after having two road bikes, bought a Harley Cruiser, met my other half through a blind date and became a mum – which I had dreamt of and which I thought at times may never happen. It really is true, you never know what is around the corner and I look forward to the adventures that await.

What is your *why*?

My driving force falls into a few different categories. Firstly, and most importantly, my family. I want to do my absolute best for them, to be a good role model for my girls and to show them that if you work hard, if you are a good person and you stay true to your values, you can achieve anything you put your mind to. I know that sounds completely cliché, and sure, there are some things that may be out of reach, for example, one of the things I wanted to do when I was younger was to become a fighter jet pilot. My short-sightedness didn't really help with that partic-ular career path. My parents worked so hard to ensure that my brother and I never missed out on anything we wanted to try and do. They were always so supportive and always wanted the best for us, even if that meant they missed out on things for themselves. I am truly appreciative of the sacrifices they made. My dad was a long-distance truck driver which inevitably meant he missed out on birthdays and school and sport presentations etc. I know that he did those things for us so that we could do our dance classes, our sports, our music lessons etc. Mum was (and still is) always there for us whether that was ferrying us to our dance classes or sports, helping us with our schoolwork etc. I want the best for my girls as well.

When it comes to my career, I think initially my driving force was proving to myself that I could do it, that I could be a partner at a top tier law firm. I am quite goal-orientated. I wasn't sure what I wanted to do when I first finished high school, but I did know that I wanted to explore the corporate world – I had always enjoyed business studies and legal studies. I didn't know when I started my law degree that I necessarily wanted to be a lawyer, but I thought that a double degree in business and law would place me in a good position for future career choices. When it became clear that I was destined to be a lawyer, I set myself a goal of working at a top tier law firm and then when I was there that I wanted to make senior associate and then partner. Intrinsically, I am a hard worker, something that I inherited from my parents, I believe. I have learnt to persevere, and I have grown to become more resilient, and it is all of these things that have helped me in my life.

Another aspect of my driving force is, I would say, part of my personality, I am stubborn and determined. If someone tells me that I can't do something, then that makes me even more determined to show them wrong. This extends to all parts of my life, whether it was my Dad and brother teasing me when I was younger saying I couldn't do this or that, I would make them show me how to do whatever it was, like operating an excavator, and proving them wrong – although with the excavator I am a much slower operator compared to both of them. There was also an incident with a sledgehammer and a sandstone retaining wall which resulted in me losing my fingernail as I insisted I could do it.

What is a challenge you have overcome?

As I sit here typing this, I am doubting whether my story is even one that is worthy, that someone would be interested in reading.

Those exact thoughts are what leads me to the challenge I want to mention. Imposter syndrome. I wouldn't say that I have completely overcome it necessarily, but rather I don't let it stop me from trying new things or taking on new challenges. I don't let it make so much noise that it stops me from trying to achieve my goals and do better. I believe almost everyone experiences imposter syndrome in one form or another, at some point in their life.

On the one hand, I see it as a positive because it ensures that I don't become complacent and that I keep on challenging myself, trying new things and not taking anything for granted. On the other hand, I need to ensure that it doesn't stop or hinder me from trying to achieve new things, from putting myself out there. It is something that I believe requires ongoing management, and a strong support network around you also helps.

I must say that I don't feel as though there is anything overly special about my story. I am hopeful, however, that my story will resonate with some and hopefully help in building some confidence to pursue your goals and make you think, *What if …?* even if you don't feel like you fit the mould. I became a partner at an Australian top tier law firm at the age of thirty-three. I did not follow what I would call the 'usual' path, but my drive, my passion and my hard work helped me to achieve my goals. I mean, really, is there such a thing in any part of our lives that is the 'usual mould' these days?

I am also a person who mostly keeps her worlds separate, and I don't like to overshare unless you are part of my inner sanctum. Not because I have anything to hide but I am just not that kind of person. As such, opening up and sharing in this book is a challenge in itself. As an over-analyser, I have gone over the words time and time again, and as a lawyer, thought how they could be interpreted this way or that way and being vulnerable to actually share this insight into my world. All in all though, I hope that at least one person, after reading this, even if they feel out of their comfort zone, even if it seems as though they might not tick all the rights boxes that are expected or that they think are to be ticked, that they can be confident in themselves and give their current challenge (whatever it might be, professionally or personally) a real hard crack – you just never know how it might turn out.

On a personal note, that's how I met my now-fiance. I met him on a blind date through a friend I met at work. Initially I was not keen on the idea – at all. Years later, we're a great team, he's one of my top supporters and we have two beautiful girls that makes me realise how lucky we are to have found one another and that surviving those first few awkward dates was all worth it. Now, to tackle the wedding plans …

What are your future plans?

This is such a good question, because for the first time in my life, I honestly don't know what my long-term future plans are, and I think that is okay for the time being. I have always had a plan – I can't actually remember a time when I didn't have one. I love a good five-year plan.

At the moment, I am working out what's next long-term. I am currently navigating my return to work with two little ones. I am enjoying reconnecting with colleagues, and clients and meeting new ones. I am loving every moment of the girls, they grow so quickly and they are at such a wonderful age – my eldest is coming out with the most hilarious things, at times her negotiation skills are mind-blowing, and my little one is learning so many new things, plus seeing the two of them interact is absolutely magical. I love hearing the two of them giggling as they are playing a game with each other. When it's too quiet, they are usually up to something mischievous together.

I am focused on trying to be a good mum and getting back into the work groove and then, when the dust has settled, I want to give myself some time to work out what is next and what I need to do to start moving in that direction. I am intrinsically an over-analyser which is a good trait to have as a lawyer, but at the same time, it can be exhausting. I remember a client telling me once to be careful not to become a deal junkie. At the time, I laughed it off but after having completed a few big deals back-to-back, I understood what he meant. You chased that next deal and were looking for the next one as soon as one closed. Don't get me wrong, I love working on those types of matters, and in reality, I do still chase that next deal but at the same time, in my industry, it is also okay to have some downtime, or perhaps this would be better worded as: it is okay for me to accept to having some downtime. I think we have to give ourselves the time and space to have the ability to reflect and work out exactly what it is we want to chase down next. As I type this, I am thinking I really should take my own advice here. Our lives are so busy with work, family, friends – we are all trying to squeeze in as much as we can every day. Everyone is quite time-poor. It is okay to take the time to reflect on what is truly important to each of us and then work out the plan to pursue that. Something else that has also become abundantly clear to me is that what works for one person won't necessarily work for someone else, we each need to pave our own paths – they may be a bit bumpy, a bit windy, but the path will still snake its way round. At the moment, my long-term path might be a little unclear but the short-term is definitely positive – whether it's spending quality time with my fiance and our girls, or chasing down that next deal, or catching up with clients, colleagues, family and friends. I look forward to cherishing this time in my life, being content, and then when the time is right, working out how the next chapter may read, what the next adventure looks like and what the action steps are going to be.

What advice would you give your thirteen-year-old self?

There are so many things I would say to my thirteen-year-old self. Overall, it would be the same advice that my mum and dad gave to me as a thirteen-year-old: if you try hard enough, you put to your mind to it, you can do anything you want to.

You don't know what your future holds.

Take all opportunities that come your way with both hands. Even if you have some preconceived idea as to what something might be like, you never really know until you have experienced it for yourself – so put aside those preconceived thoughts and go in with an open mind even if it may feel a little unknown, a little scary.

I know that I have just said to say yes to opportunities that arise, but it's important to realise it is also okay to say no – don't stretch yourself too thin – give yourself time to breathe.

We get so busy that we don't really allow ourselves the time to self-reflect or maybe we don't like to self-reflect so much. I think I have learnt to say no a bit more since becoming a mother.

It's okay to go outside of your comfort zone even if you are nervous. I am intrinsically a creature of habit – it is important to push yourself to change those things that you don't like, to the extent they are within your control, and it is also okay to try something new and for it not to work out – at least you will know that you gave it a shot and won't be thinking, *What if?*

Be informed – ask questions – continue to learn. We are all continuing to learn every single day, and as my mentor once told me, the more senior you get, the more interesting the work and things get – that is certainly very true in my industry.

There is a whole wide world out there, explore, meet new people and continue to grow. I work in the property industry and if I think back to when I was going through high school and starting university, there are so many jobs out there, career options that I didn't even know existed.

If at first you don't succeed, try again, even if that means you are not following the most direct path, if it is what you want to achieve, chase down that goal. You have to find something you enjoy doing, something you love (most days, anyway).

Form great friendships. It is not about how many friends you have, or how many likes you have, it's about those friends that you can call any time, day or night, and they will be there for you if you need them, even if life gets in the way and you haven't seen them as regularly as you would have liked.

Be genuine, trustworthy and open. Honesty goes a long way. It's okay to ask for help.

Surround yourself with good, kind people. Find great mentors/champions (I certainly did) and give back.

And never forget to be true to yourself.

ABOUT CARRIE ROGERS

Hi, my name is Carrie Rogers, and to be honest, I can't quite believe I am doing this. I must admit, I am experiencing a bit of imposter syndrome, having the opportunity to collaborate in this book with some very impressive and phenomenal women. I grew up at the bottom of the Blue Mountains at East Kurrajong and currently live in Sydney with my significant other and two gorgeous little girls. Ordinarily, my day job is as a partner in one of Australia's top tier law firms, although, as I type this, I am on maternity leave having welcomed my second daughter into the world a few months ago. Despite the current craziness in the world, as a result of the pandemic, I am absolutely loving life and spending extra precious time with my girls.

I loved growing up in East Kurrajong, noting that this appreciation really solidified once I moved to the city to be closer to work. As a kid, I may have complained that there was nothing to do, now, I cherish the open space and the quietness of it all except, of course, when I get to jump on my Harley and go for a ride away from the hustle and bustle of the city streets.

I went to school at the local primary and high school and started studying a double degree in business and law at, as it was known then, the University of Western Sydney (now WSU). When I started my degree straight out of school, I wasn't sure what I wanted to do but I enjoyed business and legal studies and thought either degree would mean I could get a job. Whilst studying at uni full-time, I also worked at the local hardware store and a small suburban law firm. After four and a half-ish years, I then scored a job as a legal secretary at the large city law firm where I have now been for over fifteen years, having worked my way through the ranks. I did take a bit of a hiatus in-house, which was fantastic, but at that time in my career, I decided I still wanted to see if the girl from the west could make partner. There was something there that I wanted to prove to myself, as well as being the type of person if I get told I can't do something, sets out to prove the naysayers wrong.

KAREN EVANS-CULLEN

M&A lawyer | Mother | Wife
Committed to supporting others to grow.

Tell us your story to now

When I think about my story, I have an overwhelming sense of how it is but a chapter in a much larger book, and one that still has many pages to be written. And it is a story that has a very strong theme of family, working hard and making the most of the opportunities that come my way.

I was born in a small country town in Western Australia, Northam, where my dad was posted for work. I am the eldest child in my family and the first granddaughter on both sides. I have a sister who is two years younger than me and like most siblings, as children, we oscillated between being the fiercest of enemies and the best of friends, often many times in one day! As adults, we are now the best of friends and have a bond that has remained incredibly strong despite living in different cities and countries for over twenty-five years.

I was blessed to have a childhood that was filled with love and support. My parents instilled in me the drive to work hard and always do my best. If you did that, they would back you

100%, proudly cheer you on, and celebrate in your successes and achievements with great pride and happiness. And when things didn't go your way, they would always be there to support and comfort you and get you back on your feet. Not much has changed, even today, although I suspect that the achievement of mine that they are most proud of are the precious grandchildren I've produced!

As a young child, we moved around several country towns in WA, but by the time I started school, we had moved to Perth. My childhood memories of that time are probably similar to many others who grew up in Australian suburbia – we roamed the neighbourhood with our friends, rode our bikes, ate ice creams and swam in our swimming pool (which made us the most popular house on the street). School holidays were trips to town to go to the movies followed by lunch at a department store, seeing cousins and family friends, picnics, playgrounds and summers at the beach. I had a lot of cousins, whose ages spanned over thirty years, and family celebrations were large in scale and occurred often.

I've always been a self-conscious person and very aware of what others might think about me and anxious to make sure their view of me aligned with how I wanted to be seen. I wanted to please and impress the adults around me, and I wanted the children to like me and trust me as the leader. I would regularly assume the leadership role in a group of children. Whether that resulted from me often being the oldest in the group, or the oldest girl, or whether that was something I was innately drawn to, I still don't know. My favourite quote from my school reports was my grade two teacher saying, 'Karen is a second little teacher in our class.' From that time on, I spent my primary school years trying to impress my teachers and win their approval, all the while saying I wanted to be a teacher when I grew up.

When I moved to high school, things changed a little. I was still highly motivated and worked hard to achieve academically. But as happens with all teenagers, I began to care less about what the adults in my life thought about me and became much more focused on winning the approval and friendship of my peers. So my high school years were spent working hard enough to achieve the academic results that had become part of who I was, but becoming less concerned about the approval of adults and much more concerned with the approval of my friends and having a wide social group.

After school, I went to the University of Western Australia, studying commerce and law. And there I found my passion; I loved studying law. At school, I'd always been really good at maths and sciences, but neither really excited me. Instead, I loved words and ideas and debate and winning arguments. In law, I could put both of these skills to work – I could take a problem, apply a wide range of rules and policies in a methodical and logical way to come up with a solution. I also loved that the solution was never black and white, right or wrong, but left room for nuance and debate. I loved the academic rigour of law, and I thrived on the camaraderie and social side of law school and university and felt a real sense of belonging.

My law school experience shaped so much of my life as it is now. Not only did it give me the wonderful career that I still enjoy and thrive in today, twenty-five years later, but it also was the place where I met and fell in love with my husband, David.

I think I can genuinely say that if I hadn't gone to law school my life would probably have borne little resemblance to what it is today. And for that reason, I remain a very grateful and loyal alumni of UWA Law School.

After law school, I worked in Perth's largest law firm and was in my element. I was able to put into practice many of the skills and knowledge I'd gained at law school. But the experience of applying that in real life for real clients to achieve real outcomes, and working as part of a team to do so, was absolutely fascinating and exciting for me. The firm was young and dynamic and driven to be the best. I was given huge amounts of responsibility across a broad range of transactions and had a huge learning curve.

But after two years, I had a strong urge to travel and see more of the world. Growing up in Perth in the seventies and eighties was what most would consider an idyllic childhood. However, Perth is one of the most isolated cities in the world and during the days before email, mobile phones and the internet had taken off, it became a rite of passage for many young people in Perth to travel overseas. I was determined that my travel would advance my career, I was loving what I was doing and not ready to have a gap year, so I decided to study for a Master of Laws. I applied for a number of scholarships and was lucky to be awarded two – one a Fulbright scholarship and the other a UWA sponsored scholarship. At the age of twenty-five, I found myself flying halfway (literally) around the world to Washington DC on a one-way ticket to study at Georgetown University. I left behind my family and my very understanding boyfriend and arrived in a country I'd never been to where I knew no-one. It was a transformative experience for me. I had to grow up and develop confidence and resilience and learn to engage with a very diverse range of people. I was studying with students from eighty-five countries and fifty states. I learnt very quickly about the Australian culture and identity and how different it was to those of most other nationalities. It was an amazing adventure for me, not only did I excel in my studies, but I had so many wonderful experiences that have forever shaped the way I view the world and my place in it.

After this amazing year, moving back to Perth immediately was not an option for me, although the long-distance relationship wasn't working for me either, so I knew that I wanted to be living in the same city as my boyfriend. We considered New York and London, but neither of those seemed to tick all the boxes. In the end, we settled on Sydney – a big city where we could experience working on big deals, live a more interesting and vibrant life outside of work, but still be close to home and in a place where we would belong and not always be different or outsiders. Our original plan was to stay for two years before returning home, but almost twenty-five years later, we're still here! Apart from the fact that our parents and siblings still live in Perth, Sydney feels very much like home to us now, particularly after the brutal WA border closures during the pandemic which have locked us out of our home state for most of the past two years.

When we arrived in Sydney in the late 1990s, I was lucky enough to almost pick up where I left off with my old law firm, although now working in the firm's biggest office (which was three times the size of our Perth office) and working for one of Australia's leading M&A lawyers. It was an exciting time for me in my career, working on some of Australia's biggest ever deals for Australia's biggest companies, coming up with innovative new deal structures and helping rewrite some of the rules around how to do those kinds of deals in this market. I had some amazing opportunities for such a young lawyer, and before I knew it, I was a partner of the firm when I turned thirty and a whole new world of opportunity and responsibility opened up for me. Becoming a partner in a law firm is a huge milestone for a private practice lawyer and it was something that I was very proud and excited to have achieved. Having said that, making partner is not the pinnacle and there is a long journey after that to fulfill the potential that the opportunity of partnership in a leading law firm provides you with.

At the same time as my career was forging ahead, so was my personal life. After seven years together, David and I married back in Perth, sharing the special day with our friends and family who came from far and wide. We bought our first home in Perth (still thinking we would eventually settle there) and then an apartment to live in in Sydney, became parents to two puppies and juggled two very busy M&A careers while trying to work out how to fit children into the picture. When our first child arrived a few years later, we realised that he was the picture, and everything else just had to fit in around that. Two years later, our second child arrived to complete our family and time flew by as we relished our busy lives, always juggling family and work and trying to find enough time in-between to keep ourselves well. For the most part, we made it work. There were certainly times when we felt overwhelmed, when the absence of any family support close by almost became too much. But we had good help, two nannies who over fifteen years became part of our family and helped us raise two happy, smart and caring children who make the juggle all worthwhile. While keeping all the balls in the air was hard, it seemed to work for us as a family and so we kept on going.

That brings me to today, I've just turned fifty, my children are teenagers and my eldest is entering year twelve. They are becoming more independent; they have their own views about the world and what they want to contribute, and they are the thing in my life I am most proud of. But with their growing independence, I've had time and space to think about my career and where I want to take it, to make some changes and take on new challenges and opportunities. After staying with one law firm for twenty-three years, I've now changed jobs twice in the past five years as I re-evaluate how my career will engage and sustain me over this next phase of my life.

What is your *why*?

It's hard for me to describe my driving force, I think it comes from a combination of factors and influences which changes in momentum and direction as those factors have waxed and waned over time. The origins of my driving force are the values that my parents instilled in me: to work hard, do your best and make the most of the opportunities that come your way. They also showed me that no matter what opportunities and experiences come along, to keep your family at the centre of everything you do because it is those relationships that will sustain and motivate you, comfort and protect you, wherever your journey takes you.

As much as my career is an extremely important part of who I am, it pales into insignificance when compared with my family. Raising children that know you want nothing but the best for them, that you will support them and have their back, and providing them a stable and loving foundation from which they can explore the world and all the opportunities available to them, has been my *why* since my children arrived in my life.

I have sought to ensure that my career does not stop them from experiencing the security and support that comes from a home life that is both nurturing and motivating. While my childhood was very different in many respects, I wanted to make sure I could replicate the fundamental foundation on which it was based, while living the life that my parents had encouraged me to aspire to. I may not have achieved the balance I wanted each and every day, but I hope my children know that there is nothing I wouldn't do to help them achieve their dreams and goals and live happy and fulfilled lives.

Having success in my career alongside my role as a parent has been really important as part of the values I want to instil in them. Having these two roles shows my children not only the importance of work and family, but also the importance of finding balance between them. It shows both my son and daughter that women can and should have the opportunity to have a fulfilling job outside the one they also have at home. It demonstrates the value of hard work, the need to balance competing demands in your life, and the satisfaction that comes from working hard at something you are good at and achieving your goals. It also shows them that the privileges we have in our lives because of our careers do not come for free and should not be taken for granted. Instead, they are the result of working hard, perseverance and making the most of opportunities that come your way. While my parents had different lives to the one I lead, these values were central to how we were raised and I hope that I am living my life in a way that instils those same values in my children. They have very fortunate lives with many privileges, and I want them to know that they are not entitled to that just because they were lucky enough to be born into this family and at this time. Instead, they need to be grateful for and earn those privileges and demonstrate that they are worthy of them. This does not, of course, mean that they cannot choose a different path in life to the ones we've taken. If that is what makes them happy and fulfilled, then I hope I have given them the confidence to do that and the grace to understand the consequences of their choices.

What is a challenge you have overcome?

The key challenge I've overcome in my working life is to succeed in what was once an almost solely male domain, as an M&A lawyer, but to do so in a way where I haven't lost my own identity and authenticity. It is the combination of these that has been my greatest challenge and it's taken me twenty years to arrive at a place where I can confidently say I've overcome both elements of this challenge.

In my early years, when I made partner at such a young age and was an integral part of a number of market-defining transactions, to do that in Sydney as a female lawyer who'd grown up in Perth – so lacked any school network, family, university or other social connections – felt like a huge challenge to overcome.

I would constantly go to meetings with boards, executives, investment bankers and other lawyers where I was the sole female in the room. All the partners I worked for were male. Most of my colleagues and peers were male. Many men and women considered that the demands of transactional work meant it was not suitable for women, especially if you wanted to have a family. But I overcame those views and became a successful M&A partner with a strong reputation in the market.

As time went on though, I realised that the successes I had achieved did not mean this challenge had been overcome. I have realised that the bigger challenge is still to be overcome, the achievements in themselves are not the end game. Instead, the real challenge is achieving all of this while not losing the essence of what is important to me and what makes me who I am. It is only fairly recently that I've been able to reflect on the first ten years or so of my career and realise that the environment in which I found myself, and what I felt I needed to do to succeed in that environment, did make me hide or suppress some of my natural strengths and inclinations. Why? I attribute it to my self-awareness, that ability to sense what matters to others and my subconscious desire to fit in and be liked and accepted. In a male-dominated environment, that requires you to become more like them, or in my case, more like what I thought men wanted to see and be around in a work environment. So, I suppressed my emotions, I became knowledgeable and interested in things that interested them, I strived to always have the answers, to be a step ahead, to work harder than any of them. I didn't try to become like them in every way, I still enjoyed and indulged in fashion, make-up and jewellery. I was always going to be different, so I made sure that those parts of me that were unavoidably different could never be criticised as not being good enough.

It was about five years ago now when I realised that for a really long time, I had been pretending to be someone that wasn't completely genuine. I wasn't being my authentic self at work. I had emphasised the thinking, analytical and driven aspects of my personality and suppressed the caring, loving and relationship driven aspects. There was no single moment which led to this revelation, but rather a combination of circumstances that over time revealed this behaviour and the reasons for it.

Becoming a mother was a significant part of the impetus for the realisation. It brought my emotions to the surface as my maternal instinct kicked in and revealed the compassionate and caring side of my personality where putting the needs of others first became second nature. I could no longer hide this side of me, it was at play every day in my life. And slowly, the person I was outside of work started to turn up to work. At the same time, I had been doing self-analysis and assessments as part of executive coaching and leadership development programs. This gave me greater insight into who my authentic self was and why I'd been hiding parts of her away.

At the same time, the external environment started to become much more open to, and began to embrace, diversity and authenticity in leadership. Suddenly, it was okay to be vulnerable, to have feelings at work, to share them with colleagues and peers and clients and my team and to care about people and your impact on them. Not only was it okay, but people now expected it of you as a leader.

The combination of these forces over time has led to me now feeling free to be my authentic self at work. What surprised me most in this process was that I had never been consciously aware that I'd adapted my personality to my environment in a way that meant I had shut down some parts and overemphasised others. I've also realised that behaviours that have developed over twenty years are hard to shift and change, however now that I have greater awareness of how I react to certain circumstances and why, I have the ability to choose when it serves me and when it doesn't.

What are your future plans?

My immediate future plans at this point involve more of the same. My family will continue to be the epicentre of all that I do. But I also see myself having much more freedom to make decisions about my career and what is important to me alongside my family as they grow up and become independent adults. That will mean I have more time for my career, more time for me and more time to give to others. Just how I might choose to do that in the future is still evolving. With over twenty-five years of experience as a corporate lawyer involved in complex and innovative deals, I have a lot to contribute, whether as an adviser, an executive or as a director.

At the moment, I am enjoying my new role, back as a partner in a law firm, and working with clients on significant and complex transactions. I have a wonderful team of lawyers working for me, who are smart, hardworking and loyal as well as a lot of fun. I enjoy watching them grow and develop and achieve the goals they set for themselves, both in their careers and personally. Being a good leader to them and helping them achieve their aspirations is a huge motivation for me in building a sustaining a successful business that they can share in.

I do want to find more time to enjoy some of the things in life that a busy career and family has made more challenging. Travel with my husband will be a big priority in the years ahead. We've spent far too long never having the right moment to visit many of the places we yearn to explore. Spending more time with my family in Perth is also a big priority – the old adage of *you don't know what you'll miss until it is gone* is very true on both these fronts. So, when the pandemic finally passes and we regain the freedom to undertake these activities without consequence, I am certainly planning to make the most of it!

What advice would you give your thirteen-year-old self?

Marry well, don't be afraid, focus on what is important to you and be yourself.

Some may question the appropriateness of the advice to marry well. Of course, not everyone needs to or wants to marry. However, if family is going to be the pivot around which your life turns, which it always was for me, then the partner you choose to create that family with is an extremely important decision. It should be someone who shares your values, who knows what is important to you and will help you achieve that. It should be someone you like and that you trust, someone that can share in your success without feeling left behind when their success is travelling a different path. Women will never achieve the equity we aspire to in our careers and our home lives unless we have a partner who truly supports that and understands they may need to make sacrifices as well to help you do that. Your marriage should be a true partnership where each gets to play to their strengths. It is a relationship that you need to nurture and invest in, it won't always be easy making it work but if you love and respect each other and have common goals, then together you can achieve more than you ever could individually.

As I started in my career, there was a lot of talk of women 'having it all'. We all now know that's a myth. Everything we choose to do means we forego something else. It's important to remember that when you choose to do something, you are choosing not to do something else. When you are making these choices, it can really help if you have clear in your mind what is important to you, as that can help you make the right decisions, choose the right things and leave behind those that don't matter to you. If you can understand what truly matters to you, or what matters the most, you are more likely to be fulfilled by the decisions you make. It's also important to keep evaluating what's important to you – that will change through your life, so make sure you are mentally checking in with where you are up to, what is fulfilling you, what is depleting you, and adjust your choices accordingly.

Don't let fear make your decisions for you. It's okay to be afraid sometimes – afraid to try, to fail, to challenge yourself, to say yes, to say no, to go, to stay. While you should listen to your fears and sometimes even let them guide the decisions you make, you should always be intentional about it. Sometimes fear can protect you, but other times it can hold you back and stop you from achieving something really great or important. It can stop you from becoming the person you want to be or having the experiences that you need to have. The best outcomes come from when we push ourselves out of our comfort zone into the place where we feel a little fear and don't know how things will eventuate, because that is how we grow.

Be yourself – some will like you, some won't, and that's okay. Trying to be someone that you are not, whether consciously or subconsciously, is exhausting and will stop you from achieving your full potential. That doesn't mean we can't try to improve ourselves or change ourselves, it means knowing who you are and working from there. I realise it's easy at my age to give this advice, after it's taken me a lifetime to be comfortable being myself and not the person my family or my friends or my colleagues or clients wanted me to be or thought I was. When you're young, your *self* is still evolving and it can be hard to recognise her, much less accept her. And to be honest, I'm still not completely there yet, it's a work in progress but when I am authentic and open, I feel like I have the best chance to live a life that really fulfills me.

ABOUT KAREN EVANS-CULLEN

My Instagram profile describes me as a 'lawyer, wife, mother (not necessarily in that order!)'. This reflects my purpose in life – to achieve a balance of success and happiness in each of these roles in a way that sustains me and then to share that with those around me so they can go on to achieve their own success and happiness.

I've been a lawyer for over twenty-five years, and in that time, I've worked on some of Australia's largest and most complex corporate deals. I love the challenge of solving complex problems and pursuing ambitious outcomes as part of a multidisciplinary team that works cohesively. When I look back at the early success in my career, it is now evident to me that much of that came despite the fact that I was female. Slowly that is changing, and it is much rarer to be the only woman in the room. I am now passionate about using my position and experience to support and provide opportunities for the other women in the room.

I've been a wife for over twenty years and am blessed to have shared most of my adult life with someone who is truly my partner in life. We share not only the same birthday, but the same values and purpose, and I could not have achieved half of what I have without him by my side.

Finally, my greatest role of all, as mother to my amazing children, my sixteen-year-old son and fourteen-year-old daughter. The intensity of my love for them is something I never expected – I would do anything for them. They fulfill me, they exhaust me, they make me swell with pride, they really do make it all worthwhile.

MELANIE POWER

Entrepreneur | Cat lover | Mother
Out-of-the-box thinker & empowerer of women.

Tell us your story to now

I think I can, I think I can, I think I can.

'Yes you can, Mel. You can do anything that you put your mind to.'

Words to me from my father at the age of seven. He had just given me my very first guitar and it was bigger than I was!

I remember picking it up, relishing the feel of the polished wood under my hands and I remember how the string pushed against and almost cut into the soft flesh of my finger (there were many blisters to come), and my hands were so small I struggled to play simple chords. But Dad's consistent words of encouragement stayed in my mind and heart from that day onwards.

I was always a girl with a spirit for doing things my way – I learned as much as I could and was prepared to put the work in to understand how to do things. I never really followed the crowd. I went to eleven schools in thirteen years due to my father being in the financial industry and being moved around with his job position (and great ones they were). So, from a young age, I had to learn to be strong in my own identity, and for most of my younger years I was always very shy – social skills were not my forte and I often found myself speaking out of turn, or stating the obvious when really I should have had more discernment. I lacked the ability to understand how to socially integrate well.

As a result of this, I was bullied incessantly – a young girl with glasses, unruly curly hair, fair skin that burned in the sun and slightly overweight. I just didn't fit in. I found that writing, music, reading and horses were my escape and I very quickly became quite adept in these areas – they were my passions.

As I reached my later years in school, my love of music and the novelty of being a female bass player in the eighties provided me with social acceptance including my quirkiness and creativity (which today is just considered the norm). I soon gained confidence and stepped into leading my own way forward – and others followed. In my high school years I changed schools every year, and by year eleven I was taking myself off to school on my first day, meeting teachers and new friends without the support of my parents. I learned very quickly that the way forward was to visit each 'clique' and get to know the people I liked, then form my own 'clique' and others soon followed into the new tenure.

I was building and leading communities and didn't even realise it. In today's world we would label that an 'influencer'. I learned very quickly to shake off harsh words and criticism and realised that these stones were only others' insecurities. I had formed my armour to survive the constant change and forge a way to maintain my own identity and strength.

Mel Power was born.

From there I moved into my passion of music and gained entrance to the Conservatorium of Music where I started a music and education degree intending to go into the teaching system. This quickly changed after several practical teaching sessions where I quickly realised that even though I loved teaching and children, the system was very institutionalised and the structure simply did not suit me. I changed degrees to business with a major in marketing ...

I had found something that would allow me to form a career with a pathway for my creativity.

My early roles were in accounting firms and I very quickly realised that I loved the ethos of small businesspeople – you see, they shared the mantra of, *I think I can, I think I can*, and I soon learned that numbers told a story and this information could be used creatively to brainstorm ideas for business, mix this with emerging technology and what a recipe! My first business was born.

Very soon I was planting, growing and selling businesses, I had found my area of genius – the foundation of numbers and the creativity of marketing – and the ability to lead and influence and SELL was the recipe. I had businesses across many sectors ... IT, accounting, bookkeeping, motorcycle dealerships, IT and computing, electronics, finance and insurance brokerages. I was an early adopter of digital marketing – it was FUN, challenging and completely fed my soul for its hunger of learning, risk-taking and the adrenalin of success and navigating challenges whilst raising my three sons too ... the fun of family and small business! (For those of you that know this well, you will understand my absolute tongue-in-cheek comment but also the pain of having to live with guilt around placing your kids in day care – it's a serious thing to deal with.)

Later in my life I was engaged with Xero accounting software company which led me to my next adventure in corporate. As their head of bookkeeping I was faced with probably the biggest test of my life, building and leading communities, public speaking, blog and article writing, and also the biggest achievement of my life, the education on business growth I birthed and created – but I was also facing the brunt of many stones being thrown (this happens often as you stick your head up – and I want to publicly acknowledge Jo Burston from Inspiring Rare Birds for walking this journey with me). I had to hone a lot of these skills on the fly, but it also was a natural progression. It was the most fun I had ever had in a role, and Xero and the people that were in it at that time will always hold a very special place in my heart, and those people are still part of my life today. It's a complete testament to the values and culture that the company was founded and built upon by Rod Drury (thanks, Rod – super fun times). It was the HARDEST I had ever worked in my life but the most fun, I mean I worked harder than I had even worked in my own business.

After almost five years in that role, it was time for me to hang up my Xero blue cape and move into what I absolutely wanted to do. Education and mentoring.

Melanie Power The Business was born.

Over five thousand students served over five major markets in two years, a team traversing the globe and women changing their lives one at a time.

I knew I could, I knew I could, I knew I could.

What is your *why*?

I have always had a heart for people that run small businesses, and in particular women that are making this journey, helping them realise that they are bigger than themselves, but also they already have everything they need within them to succeed.

Just like I did from young age.

Entrepreneurship is something that is built into some of us with an almost unbreakable spirit. It's this drive that gets us up every day – it's the *why*. If we lack a skill, then we learn it or hire someone else to do it, but the entrepreneurial spirit is something that you either have or you don't.

So my *why* is empowering women to embrace that entrepreneurial spirit and helping them to create a framework to house it so their ideas come to life and can thrive in the world. It's about self-belief, smashing the imposter syndrome and moving forward without having the spirit of perfection in the way.

I also see women often place themselves in a position of being a 'doormat' to others, in their personal lives and business. I am a big believer in leading and delivering to others with a 'heart to serve' but this comes with a price of others valuing this, and showing respect and gratitude in return. The reality is that we train others how to treat us, and if we aren't right with ourselves first, value who we are and how we can help others, then ultimately this is the energy we place out there, and intrinsically others will treat us the same way in return.

It's about learning to love who we are, embracing our own identity, valuing what we do, and then opening ourselves to walk forward to help others with this heart. It all starts with us, and working on bettering ourselves. So from this very heart of my beliefs comes my *why* of what I do …

My mantra is, *I empower women to command the life they deserve,* and this includes:

- Command the price they deserve
- Command the profit they deserve
- Command the love they deserve
- Command the [insert own word here] they deserve

What is a challenge you have overcome?

Business and life are full of many challenges and when you are faced with a mountain of shit (or a pile of poo, as I refer to it) and no gloves then it's about stepping back for a bit, assessing the situation and working out the best way to tackle it.

Here are the options:

- Hands in and start shovelling – push it up and out of the way. Fast and effective, lots of energy and stamina required.
- Do nothing. Wait for the elements to wash it away and allow a natural path to clear. Definitely a test of patience. Takes a long time, others can sometimes pass you on the path and pave the way for you to follow behind them, less risk.
- Walk around it in stealth. Safer path, takes longer, less risk but more stable way to navigate.
- Turn around, walk away and forge another path.

All of the above have one thing in common, acceptance of the situation. Before any of the strategies can be implemented, the process of acceptance has to take place and sometimes this can be quite a process, especially if you aren't used to facing challenges on a regular basis. When you are in a growth phase of your business, the challenges come thick and fast, as there are many things you are dealing with, but it's discerning which 'pile of poo' to deal with first … the thing is 'they ain't going away quickly' … so acceptance is key so you can then strategise the next move. You also need to accept that sometimes the pile takes a long time to move – it can be really drawn-out – and you have to sustain your own energy for that distance.

One of the biggest challenges I have faced recently is a business partnership that ended up not working out. It was a massive undertaking with large sums of money on the other side of the world from where I was, which meant travelling during a pandemic. It was clear there was a misalignment in values, and the effect this had on my business and me personally was immense. It took almost a full year to tackle that pile of poo (my first go-to is take the gloves off and tackle it head-on, and in this situation, this just did not work). It wasn't a clear-it-up-and-move-it, it was something that had to be traversed and navigated in a way I had not done before.

The interesting lesson for me, as a business owner, was this: taking the other option of navigating this journey allowed me a lot of time for reflection, close examination of my values, my own identity and what I stand for, and what I was here to do in life. It was a cathartic and powerful experience. I can assure you the process of acceptance took some time, and some 'foot-stamping' moments. The truth is this: something that appeared to have set me back on ALL fronts, almost forcing me back to the startup phase, only empowered me to step into the real leader I was meant to be.

Leading my company, my clients, my team, and most of all, leading others on a journey that they don't know they need to take yet …

So, when you are faced with a 'pile of poo' don't just rush on in. Take a bit of time to allow yourself to process acceptance and then strategise the next move.

You will thank your future self.

What are your future plans?

Plans for the future. A good friend asked me this not long ago and my answer was simple.

To run in the grass barefoot.

To sing like no-one is listening.

To dance like no-one is watching.

Ride more horses.

Take more walks on the beach.

Have more romantic and intimate moments with my partner.

More family dinners and board game nights.

Explore more of my 'own backyard'.

Be intentional about good food and wine experiences.

Write more books … ficton and non-fiction.

Be a crack email marketer (I mean FB is so yesterday, right?).

Fulfill my innate need to always be on the edge and going against the grain (I do love a good bit of disruption).

And … to build a life where I can do things I love and still be of service to others. Being selective about WHO I work with, I want to enjoy that process and experience it.

But also without having to be in the 'spotlight' all the time or feeling like I have to be super accessible or visible (I spent years doing this for various jobs and its time is over – I can be of extreme value to others, without having to do the DOING or LEADING in a physical way).

The recipe is simple: at fifty, I have started, run, closed and sold many businesses, worked in corporate and built others' businesses, so now it's time to build my own life around the values and activities and people I hold dear.

Being present is the thing.

Time is not endless, it's finite and I am sure I am going through that moment when you get to middle age and it hits you, *OMG, time is running out, I need to slow down and just BE.*

It's sheer gold. Gratitude is present every day for me. Even in lockdowns and the pandemic challenges we face, I still am grateful for what I have and my situation.

What advice would you give your thirteen-year-old self?

Advice to our younger selves is always full of hindsight, and we can never really have that until we have already walked the road, navigated many 'piles of poo' and been honed and shaped from the experience of life.

The truth is my younger self would have said, *Go away, I know better,* and, *I am going to conquer the world,* and a bit of, *What do you know?*

ABOUT MELANIE POWER

Melanie Power is a serial entrepreneur, having had a range of businesses from accounting and bookkeeping firms, motorcycle dealerships, finance brokerages and IT consultancy to a global education business based out of Australia, New Zealand and the USA.

Her passion and expertise are all about the planting and growing of businesses and she has developed her own unique methodology of doing this, with a specific focus on empowering women to be the master of their own destinies, to live life to their own plan and design a business that serves them and their clients!

Mel is the creator of the highly successful global movement Bookkeeper Revolution and has mentored and coached thousands of women all over the world helping them to command the price they deserve for the value they deliver!

Mel is an avid cat lover and fosters kittens for a local cat shelter, loves a good Hunter Valley wine and is passionate for Australian-made fashion!

Social handle: @themelpower

ANNICK DONAT

ASX CEO | Mother | Mentor
Advocate for financial advice and wellbeing.

Tell us your story to now

I grew up in Melbourne and life had quite a few challenges. I'm the eldest of three children, followed by a brother and sister. I was born on the tropical island of Mauritius. A tiny and beautiful island which is known for its stunning white beaches, great food and generous, kind people. My godfather tells a story that on the day I was born, there were riots in the streets of Port Louis, the capital. He was in the police force and kept saying to his fellow policemen – 'My niece has just been born, we've got to keep the streets safe and the riot away from her.' Little did I know then that my life would be faced with constant challenges and traumas which have shaped who I am today.

Mum and Dad sailed to Australia when I was about two years old. My brother was only one year old, and my sister not yet conceived. I don't remember much of my early years because they were traumatic and filled with violence and anger. It's taken years of therapy and counselling to deal with my early childhood – facing into some very scary, and at times, almost crippling memories – and to get a place where I can talk about it as my past, but it no longer defines my future.

Despite this, I was fortunate enough to be surrounded by cousins who made sure my siblings and I were looked after when home went pear-shaped and we needed somewhere to sleep and someone to look after us. I didn't realise it at the time, but there is this innate instinct of protection that kicks in when you're the oldest. From the age of five, I started protecting my brother and sister from the ugliness in our house. I remember Mum leaving us when I was very young – the house was filled with sadness and anger all at once. My dad was angry, my grandparents sad and angry, and I remember the three of us crying, not knowing what had just happened, or more importantly, where our mum had gone. I knew then it was up to me to ensure my siblings felt safe and had some direction.

This meant I had to make decisions very early in life, such as which parent to live with (I was nine), and how to deal with the anger at home whilst living with Dad, which seemed to be happening all the time. I also had to be the one who helped pack up our things the day Mum came to get us. I remember that day distinctively. I woke up and Dad wasn't home. I asked my grandmother where he was and she said, 'He's gone to kill himself because you don't want to live with him.' It's taken thousands of dollars of therapy to deal with that one … There are so many dark memories about my childhood and sometimes I wonder how on earth I made it to the life I live today, filled with love, a great family and the support of beautiful girlfriends.

I'm thankful my mother had a profoundly positive influence in my life, by encouraging me to be the best person I could be.

She was beautiful inside and out. She had an energy which drew people to her, and she was the Aunty my cousins went to when they needed advice or help. Despite it being tough financially at home, she always made sure we were well cared for. She was a great cook ... a skill she's passed on to all three of us. Nearly every Sunday afternoon, she'd make pumpkin scones, and as if by scent alone, one of my favourite cousins would turn up, salivating as they came out of the oven piping hot! Once the butter was melted, the scones were devoured. Thankfully my sister and niece have mastered the art of making them, so the legend lives on.

At the age of forty-four, my mother collapsed from a brain aneurysm, leaving her incapable of caring for herself. I was twenty-one at the time. It was one of the worst days of our lives. My siblings and I had moved out of home by this time. It was a Saturday afternoon and we'd been out most of the day. I got home before everyone else and was waiting in the driveway to get into the house we were renting. I'd forgotten my keys, and there were no mobile phones ... I could hear the phone in the house ring, then stop, then ring again, then stop, then ring again ... I knew something was wrong, but I could never have imagined it the way it unfolded.

When my siblings arrived home, they were with some of my cousins. One of them rushed inside to the phone, answered it and I remember seeing all the colour drain out of their face ... I still can't remember who answered the phone ... I don't think any of us do. All I remember is hearing, 'Mum's collapsed, she's been rushed to St Vincent's Hospital in Melbourne. Meet us there, but don't let Annick drive.' I was yelling at them asking so many questions that no-one could answer. No-one knew if

Mum was alive. When we got to hospital, Mum had been rushed into intensive care and they were waiting for a neurosurgeon to arrive. While we were at the hospital, there were three moments that stood out.

The first was a doctor coming out and saying, 'Your mum's brain has a lot of swelling, but her body temperature is too high [it was over forty degrees], so we have to wait till the swelling goes down and her temperature drops … we not sure she's going to make it.'

The second was being allowed into intensive care, my siblings were too distraught to see her … standing next to her bed, tears streaming and a nurse asking, 'Is this your sister?'

I managed to get out, 'She's my mother.'

The third was being asked whether we wanted to turn off the life support because Mum was in a coma and the doctors didn't think she was going to make it through the night. I now understand the 'sliding doors' moment and the impact split-second decisions make when life is in turmoil. I wanted to turn off the machine. Mum had always told us that if she couldn't look after herself, then she didn't want anyone else to. She had the most amazing long, shiny black hair and she took very good care of it. She often told my sister and me that she never wanted to be in a situation where someone else brushed her hair. The doctors told us that if she did survive, her quality of life would be very poor. None of us wanted that for her but making the decision to turn off life support is not one anyone should have to make … and we were twenty-two, twenty and eighteen. To make it worse, we had a dozen other family members in the room who were all distressed and trying to tell us 'kids' what to do. I will always be grateful to my cousin Colette, who said, 'You can't let her die like this, she wouldn't want that.'

We didn't turn off the life support, Mum made it through the night and whilst her quality of life ended that day, she lived long enough to see two of us get married and meet four of her grandchildren. It took a long time for me to deal with the guilt of seeing her living in a nursing home from such a young age. I always questioned if we (I) had made the right decision. But watching her hold her grandchildren for the first time or watching her laugh with them when they visited the nursing home and being able to celebrate some Christmases and birthdays together, made me realise she was meant to live to see this – to meet them and they her.

Mum passed away in 2016, and all four grandchildren spoke at her funeral. Life has a way of sending you the moments you need to experience. Watching our kids, my niece and nephew supporting each other as they read their messages of love to Nanna had such a profound effect on me. It was the right sliding door.

Many of the things Mum taught me have shaped the woman and leader I am today. She taught me so much when I was a teenager – she had this joy for life and adventure and encouraged us to live our best lives. My favourite piece of advice I received from Mum was as a teenager when she said to me, 'Be smart, be feminine and trust your instincts.' She encouraged a love of learning, reading and experiencing new things. She wanted all of us to explore our potential, work hard and achieve the best results we could. As the eldest, there was a lot of pressure on me to perform well at school (Mum was a teacher back in Mauritius). I loved learning, and getting good marks came easily which made report card days pretty cool because of my grades. Mum always celebrated our successes. She'd make cakes, or in my case a new outfit from a piece of fabric I'd found at the local Spotlight remnant bin! However, what stands out the most is the way she encouraged me to stand up for myself, to lead, to strive for more and to understand knowledge and learning are gifts not to be taken for granted.

Mum was an incredible seamstress; we didn't have much money to buy clothing, but she always found enough fabric to make sure we had nice clothes for functions and events. She wanted me to be proud of being female and feminine, which included 'dressing like a girl'!

The final part of these words of wisdom from her were, 'Choose your men carefully.' It was her way of saying 'respect yourself'. I haven't always got that bit right … but I got there!

I have carried these words with me ever since and continue to share them with women I coach and mentor. This advice has served me well, especially when building my career in financial services.

My sister shares a story that from a very early age, I carried around a 'briefcase' filled with papers and a bright yellow toy calculator. It appears the universe had me destined for a career in financial services. I caught the 'bug' in March 1987, my first job in financial markets working in foreign exchange, stocks and bonds. I remember loving the pace at which things happened in the markets – despite having to fill out paper forms and faxes, everything seemed to move fast. The people I got to meet were interesting and had so many stories to tell, I was learning from those more experienced than me (today, still one of my favourite ways to learn), and the volume of money we traded was more than I could ever imagine.

Later that year in October, I experienced my first financial market correction. It was both exciting and terrifying. The loss wasn't just money, people were losing jobs, and in a couple of instances, their lives. It was then I began to realise the importance of planning for the unexpected, the implications of greed, and the value of understanding money and financial decisions and how it affects people and families.

Since that day, every role I've held has been focused on transferring knowledge about financial and business decisions. I've worked in all parts of the financial markets and loved all my experiences. However, about twenty years ago I was fortunate to have a role working with and supporting self-employed financial advisers. Mark Twain once said, 'The two most important days in your life are the day you are born and the day you find out why.' The moment I started working with financial advisers, I knew this was how I would spend the rest of my career. I believe great advice changes lives; I've seen the difference it can make to the financial future of families.

Family is important to me, probably because growing up, mine was so fractured and distressing (and money was scarce). Because of my challenging childhood, I had decided not to get married or have children. But it turned out the universe had other plans for me … and I'm grateful I listened! I am now blessed with a husband who encourages me to pursue my career passion, is my source of wisdom and catches me when I fall (which has been often!). Together with our two gorgeous children, we're creating the family life which eluded me as a child. Sitting at the table at dinner time and listening to our kids express their opinions and share their stories is a great reminder of the power of family.

Financial wellbeing and family stability tend to go hand in hand. Doing what I do every day allows me to shape and lead a company which educates families about understanding their money and financial decisions. It makes my role incredibly rewarding.

What is your *why*?

From a very young age, I've always been curious and adventurous about life. So, I guess my *why* is driven by making the most of every moment and opportunity where I can learn, explore, and get deep into something that has meaning and purpose. At the age of twelve (or perhaps even earlier) I became fascinated by the financial markets and in particular, the New York Stock Exchange. I wanted to know what it felt like to walk on the trading floor, surrounded by ticker tape, watching the traders call out deals at a rapid pace, seeing the 'chalkies' writing the numbers on the boards and experiencing the ringing of the bell. It all sounded very exciting, and as I was a girl who got bored very easily, this seemed like the perfect way to ensure boredom didn't set in when I grew up and went to work.

It wasn't until the 1987 stock market correction that I realised how fragile financial markets can be, and the impact on people's lives when it goes wrong. On that fateful day in October 1987, I experienced my first (of many), stock market corrections. I was twenty years old, and as I walked into the office, there was chaos everywhere. People looked shocked, frantically trying to figure out the next move, who to call, what action to take. But in-between there was an eerie silence. It quickly became clear to me that Australia, and the world, had changed dramatically in what seemed like an instant. I remember watching the news, seeing Rene Rivkin being interviewed and saying, 'This is a disaster ...'

The days and weeks that followed is where the real lessons were learned. Many friends and clients lost their jobs, homes and marriages. But one moment stands out above all – learning that one of my peers had taken his life at the age of twenty-two. He had over-extended himself in his share portfolio, lost a lot of money and for some reason decided the only way through was to take his life. The news was both shocking and heartbreaking. It was then I made the decision to find roles where we helped educate people about their money. When my mum collapsed, she had no insurance in place. It would have made a significant difference to her life if she had been insured. Of that, I'm certain – having seen and heard so many stories where having an insurance policy in place meant clients had no financial worry while they were recuperating.

Since then, I've lived and worked through many financial market corrections. Each time there's been a moment, an experience, a story that has left an indelible mark on my heart. Over the years, it's driven me to work with companies who want to help others live better financial lives. At every company, I've helped shape the way we educate, share, storytell and deliver financial advice to Australians. In our team we often say, 'Great advice changes lives,' and it does. I've witnessed it often, seen families better off because they had the benefit of speaking to an adviser who took the time to teach, guide and provide the benefit of their expertise to help people make informed decisions about the way they manage their money. And it's not just about the money … it's putting food on the table, being able to give yourself or a member of your family access to health or support when they're in need, it's having access to someone who will answer questions the next morning, when you've been awake at night thinking, *Can I pay the school fees/mortgage/rent?* or, *Will I have enough money to live on as I get older and want to retire?* … or simply … *Can I retire?* I believe in the power of financial advice; I have from the time I was twenty-two years old and had my first experience listening to a client thank their adviser for making it easier to understand their superannuation. Deciding whether to become a financial adviser was another 'sliding door moment'. I chose not to because I knew I had so much more to learn. Instead, I've had to quote Sheryl Sandberg, 'a jungle gym career' in financial services.

At every career turn, I've been blessed to work with great advisers from all generations; whether it's helping them build their small businesses or ensuring they have access to the support and resources they need to help their clients or leading a company and community of like-minded advisers who believe they exist to help and serve others to make better financial decisions.

I believe I chose the path already chosen for me. I've been able to share my passion for advice and advisers with so many people across our industry. I've become a respected voice at the table when it comes to changing regulations, new ways of giving advice or simply helping those outside the industry understand the power of great advice. I believe so much – I married an amazing financial adviser! The way Simon cares for his clients and has done for thirty years is extraordinary. It's very similar to the way he cares for our family … teaching Gus and Liv (our kids) from an early age about saving, the value of money and the impact of making decisions with their (pocket) money.

What is a challenge you have overcome?

I opened my story by sharing the trauma of my early childhood and the challenges I faced when Mum collapsed from an aneurysm. These were highly emotional and frightening experiences because I was not equipped to make some of the decisions and I had others I was responsible for keeping safe … and at the time, I was still a child.

I once read, 'If you're going through hell, keep going.' It's an extreme expression, but at its heart it's a way of saying … *Keep moving, find a way through and trust that you'll get to the other side.* When my children were little, we used to read/sing the nursery rhyme, *We're Going on a Bear Hunt* to them. My favourite part of the rhyme still to this day is, 'We can't go over it, we can't go under it – we've got to go through it!'

Aurelius said, 'The impediment to action advances action. What stands in the way becomes the way.' Whether it's a quote, a nursery rhyme, or the wisdom of a great emperor; facing into the obstacles we face daily, trusting that you have the strength and experience to make decisions, pivot, fail, get back up and you'll find a way through – I've come to learn over many years and obstacles is what shapes leaders and brings us closer to our purpose.

In late January 2020, we'd just returned home from a wonderful family holiday skiing in Italy. I'd had some health issues during 2019, not had a real break for two years, and this was a much needed and very welcomed break. I came back to work feeling refreshed, energised and ready to take on 2020. Within ten days of being back at work, our parent company was forced into administration, within four days after that, the company I led as CEO was placed on the market for sale by receivers because it was a profitable asset, and one of the creditors was (rightfully) trying to recover some of the money owed. It was only the first week in February and our (my team, our adviser community and their clients) lives changed instantly ... and then COVID-19 hit our country. As I said to the team at the time, 'We're not in Kansas anymore!'

True leadership is tested when 'the bear gets in the way of where you're going'. In good times, it's easier to lead, and whilst it may still have its moment, what defines you as a leader is how you lead yourself and others in times of crisis. For us, this was a crisis, one we thought was mainly out of our control. Receivers have one job to do: get the best price for the asset they are selling. Everything else (like people's fears) comes second, if at all. I was the CEO, the leader, the person who had to make the decisions, answer the questions, find a way through. So, what do you do when you're faced with a crisis, a global pandemic and limited decision-making power? I'm not sure there is an answer to the question, but I'll share what I did.

Within forty-eight hours, my team and I had called every adviser in our community and communicated everything we knew at the time. We let them know we would take calls any time and as soon as we understood what was happening and when, it would be shared. We kept that promise throughout the entire sales process. I emailed the community every day, even when there was nothing new to share (because I promised we would). Every week we held a teleconference, providing a forum for advisers to ask any question in a safe and transparent environment (some information couldn't be put in writing). When asked a question, I answered truthfully and with clarity. Where I didn't or couldn't provide the information, I told them as such. My team acted in the same way, with the same clarity and openness. Because of this, we had advisers saying they trusted we had their (and their clients') best interests front of mind. They became our biggest supporters and advocates. We had advisers checking in, making sure we were getting enough rest or support. We selected a key group of advisers who were tasked with representing their peers and created a culture where they could be part of the sales process from beginning to end (completely unheard of in our industry). During all of this, we were navigating the decisions of others; the government's response to COVID-19, the receivers preparing our business for sale, the competitors trying to raid, the administrators shutting down parent support and assistance … a story for another day. Supported by my incredible husband and amazing team, I quickly learned that I could only control my decisions. Aurelius' 'the impediment to action becomes the action' became my inspiration, and I immersed myself into learning the law relating to administration and receivership; I appointed a lawyer to protect our company, independent of all legal teams; I sought out help from industry peers I respected and trusted; and together with my team, we navigated a successful transaction to the company I now lead as group CEO.

There's an African proverb which epitomises the strength of working together; 'If you want to go fast, go alone. If you want to go far, go together.' We got to the other side of this crisis because of many.

The consulting team who brokered the sale, worked ridiculously hard to make sure we had a competitive market opportunity.

The receivers, we now call friends – despite a rocky start. They trusted me and my team, respected our expertise and experience, which helped the sale process immensely.

The shareholders who engaged the receivers stayed true to their word, providing support even though they had no legal obligation to do so.

Our adviser community who made sure we stuck together, because they knew this would be the best outcome for everyone.

The courage and conviction shown by my team every single day, despite the uncertainty of the outcome. There may not have been a job on the other side, especially during a global pandemic. And yet, they chose to stay together and help wherever they were needed.

During all the chaos, tears and uncontrollable moments, Simon, my wonderful husband, was the best sounding board I've ever had. He kept me grounded and caught me when I fell.

I learned a lifetime of lessons in 2020. Lessons of leadership, vulnerability, fear, self-awareness, courage, conviction and the power of believing this was my obstacle, my bear hunt to go through, because it is part of my life's purpose.

What are your future plans?

Late last year, I engaged a new coach. I've worked with coaches for years and selected them based on what I felt I needed at the time. Sometimes it's working with a business coach, or a life/spiritual coach, and other times it's working with a psychologist to deal with the emotional and mental challenges working in a male-dominated, rapidly shifting, hardcore industry, trying to find some form of 'balance'. The coach I have today focuses on 'inner work'. By the end of 2020, I was physically and emotionally spent. The company I led for went through a very public sale, we were in the middle of a global pandemic, the financial markets had crashed (again) and in my personal life, we had knocked down our house and moved into an apartment … facing lockdown for many weeks. It was also the year my dad died, and being the eldest, he had selected me as the executor. I had ridden many emotional roller-coasters – I felt lost and needed to reassess. I ascribe to the philosophy that if you ask the right questions, the universe will provide the answers. One day, I happened to be speaking to a client on the phone and noticed the *change* in him. He was focused, very clear about the direction his business needed to take, but what struck me the most was his sense of calm and contentment whilst he was sharing his future goals. It piqued my curiosity, leading me to ask what had created the change, which was so visible, even over the phone. He mentioned he'd been doing an 'inner work' program with a coach and going through the process had helped him clear the fog, make some hard decisions and it was working! Hearing the calmness of the way he deliberately spoke each sentence triggered something inside me and I knew this was what I was looking for … a way towards contentment.

It took me a long time to realise that who I am is enough, and even when I'm not sure of myself, feeling confused or scared, it's going to be okay. Because I am enough. I've spent my life setting goals, working furiously (and at times to the detriment of those I care about most, or my personal wellbeing) to achieve them, to prove that I can.

The benefit of living life this way for over five decades is that you have a plethora of wisdom to refer to when you're stuck for answers! I have many plans, and they all start and end with living my very best life, surrounded by people I love and am loved by, working with people I respect and admire to learn with and from; respecting my voice and using it for my life's purpose, a voice for change and empowering others to be better prepared for their financial future. I want to be the best leader I can, helping those who work with me feel inspired to be a better version of themselves, to take risks with the knowledge, no matter the outcome, experiencing the excitement or fervour of putting themselves 'out there'.

For me, real success comes from knowing I lived a life fulfilled, loved my husband and our children with an open heart, supported my friends and family in times of need and been their cheerleader when they were conquering the world. I'm fortunate to have found a special tribe in the Global Girls, a place where I can share thoughts, reach out for support, lend a hand when needed or just be in a 'safe space' when I'm seeking moments of quiet contemplation.

As for my career, my aspiration is to be the CEO who forged

a way where all Australians have access to quality and affordable advice. Whether they choose to do it themselves, or with the help of an adviser, there's a way to get the information and education they need to make the best possible decisions for themselves and their families. As a leader, I want to help the next generation of leaders get to where they are going faster. There are so many intelligent, passionate and courageous young leaders in my industry who see a different future for us. It's time we helped them become the leaders they are destined to be, creating a future we are yet to imagine.

What advice would you give your thirteen-year-old self?
I love the movies! I love getting lost in a story, finding myself in a world so different to mine, being on the edge of my seat in a thriller or trying to solve the mystery before the ending. Imagination is a gift and in movies, you are transformed in a way you can let your imagination run.

Over the years, I've 'collected' my favourite movie quotes, using them in presentations about life and leadership. If I was giving advice to my thirteen-year-old self, this is what I'd share.

'Life moves pretty fast. If you don't stop and look around once in a while, you could miss it.'

From the cult classic *Ferris Bueller's Day Off.*
Time moves so quickly. Before you know it, you're an adult and expected to be something or do something with your life. In corporate life, you get on the hamster wheel and only get off when you've run out of steam or spun off by a force outside of

your control. To that wide-eyed thirteen-year-old, I'd say make moments count when you can. Take the time to be curious, seek out adventures, be silly, laugh, cry and scream at life when stuff happens.

'Do or do not. There is no try.'

The great Yoda in *The Empire Strikes Back.*

Fear can be crippling for many. The adrenalin kicks in, you become conscious of *Who's watching, what will other people think, what if I make a fool of myself?* Having a go at things that scare you opens your mind, creates new neural pathways which harness your 'fight or flight' instincts. Our brains are wired to take the path of least resistance, but greatness comes from doing great things.

'E.T. phone home.'

E.T. the Extra-Terrestrial – self-explanatory.

Stay connected to those you love. Find your home – your place where no matter what's happening around you, there's a sanctuary, a safe space. For me, it's my family. For others it could be a close group of friends or a community group. No matter who or where it is, keep coming back to check in occasionally, regroup and then head off into the wild again!

'You only are free when you realise you belong no place
— you belong every place — no place at all. The price is
high. The reward is great.'

And finally, this is from the enigmatic Maya Angelou. A woman who lived a life of passion, challenge, authenticity and vision.

It's tough trying to figure out who you are or want to be when you're thirteen. It can be tough at any age. Women, in particular, always seem to be reinventing themselves. I've done it dozens of times. These profound words from Maya are a reminder to look within and be proud of who you are and who you're yet to become. Take care of the voice inside your head and hush it when it's telling you you're not enough. Appreciate your uniqueness, and the energy you create just by being on the planet. At every turn and twist along this road we call life … love who you are, right in the moment you're being you.

ABOUT ANNICK DONAT

I grew up in Melbourne and life had quite a few challenges. I'm thankful my mother had a profoundly positive influence in my life, by encouraging me to be the best person possible. At the age of forty-four, she collapsed from a brain aneurysm, leaving her incapable of caring for herself (she passed away in 2016). I often reflect on the lessons she taught me and who she would want me to be. The best advice I received from mum, was as a teenager, when she said to me, 'Be smart, be feminine and trust your instincts.' I have carried this with me ever since, and I continue to share it with women I coach and mentor. This advice has served me well, especially when building my career in financial services.

My sister shares a story that from a very early age, I carried around a 'briefcase' filled with papers and a bright yellow toy calculator. It appears the universe had me destined for a career in financial services. I caught the 'bug' in early in 1987, my first job in financial markets working in foreign exchange, stocks and bonds. I remember loving the pace at which things happened in the markets, despite having to fill out paper forms and faxes, everything seemed to move fast. The people I got to meet were interesting and had so many stories to tell, I was learning from those more experienced than me (today, still one of my favourite ways to learn) and the volume of money we traded was more than I could ever imagine.

That was March 1987. Later that year in October, I experienced my first financial market correction. It was both exciting and terrifying. The loss wasn't just money, people were losing jobs and in a couple of instances, their lives. It was then I began to realise the importance of planning for the unexpected, the implications of greed and the value of understanding money and financial decisions and how it affects people and families.

Since that day, every role I've held has been focused on transferring knowledge about financial and business decisions. I've worked in all parts of the financial markets and loved all my experiences. However, about twenty years ago, I was fortunate to have a role working with and supporting self-employed financial advisers. Mark Twain once said, 'The two most important days in your life are the day you are born and the day you find out why.' The moment I started working with financial advisers, I knew this was how I would spend the rest of my career. I believe great advice changes lives; I've seen the difference it can make to the financial future of families.

Family is important to me, probably because growing up, mine was so fractured and distressing (and money was scarce). Because of my challenging childhood, I had decided not to get married or have children. It turned out, the universe had other plans for me … and I'm grateful I listened! I am blessed with a husband who encourages me to pursue my career passion, is my source of wisdom and catches me when I fall (which has been often!). Together with our two gorgeous children, we're creating the family life which eluded me as a child. Sitting at the table at dinner time and listening to our kids express their opinions and share their stories is a great reminder of the power of family.

Financial wellbeing and family stability tend to go hand in hand. Doing what I do every day allows me to shape and lead a company which educates family about understanding their money and financial decisions. It makes my role incredibly rewarding.

NERINA LAHOUD

Property developer | Wife | Mother
Striving for perfection one day at a time.

Tell us your story to now

Born into a loving Italian family, I was enshrined in the traditional values of a melting pot of Australian and European cultures. My brother and I grew up in a strict environment, in my childhood I was oblivious to the differences between the various cultures. In my teenage years I began to feel the weight of those differences as I was missing out on memorable moments such as movies with friends, dances and school excursions, activities that the average teenager would enjoy. Luckily for me, I had a wonderful group of friends and family, many of whom had similar upbringings.

During my younger years, crucial values were instilled into my character, one of which was an unbreakable work ethic derived from my father's hardworking nature. A perfectionist in everything he put his mind towards, combined with pride in his work, my father was an inspirational figure in my life, whom many looked up to. Thus, from a young age, I observed what I could from the daunting world around me and I learnt to always do something right the first time around, and be proud of the outcome.

One of the many things I am forever grateful for was the regular holidays to Italy, some with my family and others with friends. Once I finished high school, I went on to study a business course and soon after started work with a finance company in the Sydney CBD. I started as a secretary in the finance department of the property division, moving onto looking after all the word processing personnel in NSW, and finishing as the PA for the managing director. This is where I eventually met my husband.

Despite my parents always wanting me to study a business-related course, my passion was always in fashion and I eventually enrolled in a fashion design course at TAFE in East Sydney. Despite completing that course and graduating, I remained in finance for the following ten years, working alongside several notable people and extracting many life-changing lessons along the way – lessons which shaped who I became. Unfortunately, I never got into fashion, as my parents always discouraged me and said I would be better off staying in the ever-growing industry of finance with its numerous attractions. My only regret is that I did not follow my heart and pursue my dream in the fashion industry. But, I believe the divergence of paths is always for a reason and we must look at the brighter side of things. If I had pursued fashion, I would not have met the love of my life who later became my husband.

During this time, I also helped in my family's deli on weekends, where my father again instilled his infectious industriousness. I recall his words of, 'I don't care about your work during the week, while you work here for me you put 100% in – with a smile – and at the end of the day you will be paid well.' I often reflect upon that memorable part of my upbringing. My father, may he rest in peace, was tough but fair. He taught us to do the right thing and do it with pride.

With long hours and minimal rest, my mind would struggle to leave the realm of my work, and I began to realise there are no shortcuts to get to your goals – if you really want to achieve something you must outwork those around you and sacrifice things that may obstruct this ideology. However, something which took me a long time to envisage was a work-life balance, where you must begin to be comfortable in your own abilities and what you have accomplished. Traditional values engulfed in the heart of my Italian heritage, passed down through my parents, was the importance of family, where on Sundays we would religiously take time away from our bustling surroundings and enjoy doing things together. Far beyond my years, I came to a realisation that people change and often come and go from your life, but it is important to carry the same values of trust and loyalty, because those worthy of your love will certainly stay close. Despite my competitive attitude, I am always the first to celebrate the accomplishments of those around me.

After ten gruelling yet rewarding years in finance, I went on to work for my husband's property development company, where we have now been working together for the past twenty-five years. Working beside him, my prior views of perfection and grit were reformed, with the firsthand view of buildings being constructed from the ground up of the highest quality, still infectious with character, and subsequently selling for record prices. That is what perseverance and determination translates to – to insist that the contractors perform to a high standard no matter the time or money spent, because the right clients will always appreciate quality. Despite people's attitude during the development process, that of both confusion and astonishment to the minor details that are required to be adhered to, nothing but respect is seen after the project is complete, as even they have learnt what true workmanship consists of. To say I have learnt from the best is an understatement, I take great pride in my work and always have as it has gained me great respect which makes it all worthwhile.

Moreover, I went on to study real estate in the evenings and received my licence, all whilst balancing work commitments during the day. This also motivated me to sell property in one of my husband's projects, I enjoyed this process and it gave me such satisfaction to sell a product that I believed so much in and to see the purchaser be just as excited. Working gave me a sense of purpose, stability and a satisfaction that kept me driven and motivated to always be in the best frame of mind. I have always treated people with kindness and respect, no matter what, and I have always believed it's important to be a decent person – whether it's to your staff, a potential client or in general – because, believe me, the way you treat people will leave a lasting impression.

The greatest gifts in my life are my two beautiful sons who bring me so much joy and I am forever grateful and proud of them. Coordinating my office hours to be around my children, I made sure I kept my promise to always spend time with them. I could never have imagined how having my two sons would impact my life in so many ways. I learn from them every day and I look at them and am immensely proud of the young men they have become. Every decision that I make is not made without putting them before myself. That is what unconditional love is.

It has taken years to understand the meaning of balance between work and family life. It's not easy to put this into play when you work with your husband, as trying to separate the two has been difficult at times. How can you separate having a bad day at the office and then going home and being a totally different person, when the person you live with is the boss of your work? Its not the simplest of tasks. But with experience, sometimes tears and frustration, I can honestly say I feel comfortable in myself and can balance the two as best as I can. I have also selfishly cut down on my days so I can finally have some personal time.

I am grateful for the lessons I have learnt from my late father, as well as from my husband and my brother, who continue to run successful businesses. Do what you love, do it right and respect those around you, because even though you may be the owner or director of the company, your staff are the heart and foundation of the business. Never become complacent, as this is one of the many causes of failure for many companies in their early stages. You need to constantly challenge yourself.

But the man I owe my entire gratitude is my husband, an encyclopaedia of knowledge that taught me lessons and continues to do so. To watch someone with a brilliant mind at work and learn from them is an experience I have been lucky to indulge in, sitting in the front row taking notes in my own mind and doing my best to apply them in real life. Watching and learning, being onsite in my five-inch heels, watching buildings grow from the ground up with such passion, and at times watching walls come down because they were not completed to an acceptable standard – taught me to be vigilant in seeking to achieve perfection.

I am forever grateful for my inner circle of friends, friends that have been by my side for over thirty years, strong beautiful women who I have learnt so much from and who I love and adore. My family who continues to teach me compassion, love and strength, I am forever grateful to them. My beautiful mother who continues to teach me lessons both in a traditional light and a modern context, and her strong will and perseverance is like no other.

I used to conceal an unpleasant trait – call it southern Italian stubbornness. I used to hold resentment, whether it was something said about me or my family, and I would keep that bottled up for long periods. That resentment would manifest itself into a poison, often belittling my self-worth. My husband taught me that holding onto that bitterness would often destroy me, rather than the person who caused it. Never let the small things get in your way. As long as you know who you are and where you want to be, the rest will follow. Faith and karma will take care of the rest.

Throughout this beautiful and sometimes difficult life, I have learnt how to remain true to myself and to capitalise on the lessons obtained from my beautiful mother and the two colossal men in my life; my late father and my husband. Upon reflection of my life's journey to this point, I continue to live by my mother's motto, who to me is the epitome of classic elegance and unconditional love. Grateful and humbled in the position I stand,

I am genuinely excited for what is to come.

What is your *why*?

Strength, courage, faith, perseverance, to be able to see beauty in others, to support each other, to be proud of the ones we love and their achievements, are all central values engraved into my personality.

My *why* – my driving force – to achieve the best I possibly can is infused in my work, as a woman, mother, wife, daughter, sister, sister-in-law, aunty and friend. I want to be able to teach my children that with a solid set of standards and principles, the future is at your doorstep, and despite the inevitability of sacrifice, you must love and believe in yourself. This is what drives the vigour that engulfs my assertiveness, where in the words of the great Oprah Winfrey, 'The greatest discovery of all time is that a person can change their future by merely changing their attitude.'

Watching for years how my parents worked day and night to build their own empire gave me the strength to work hard, collect my funds and buy my own piece of real estate at twenty-three. That first deposit, that first journey of my investment portfolio, was an accumulation of all the values and lessons I'd learnt, and provided me the necessary hunger to strive forward.

I don't believe in cutting corners to achieve results because sometimes the lessons extracted from the journey may prove to be more valuable than the end product.

Personally, reflecting on your childhood years is very important – to see what your parents sacrificed for you to succeed and flourish keeps you grounded and motivated. As a parent and a businesswoman, retrospect is pivotal in my driving force to be a good leader for my children, and hopefully one day I can guide them to be leaders themselves.

Where many aspects of the human experience are also reflected in the entrepreneurial world, respect and honesty go hand in hand. Coming to work for my husband in his property development company taught me another type of driving force – watching and learning how he would conduct his operations with such precision and perfection. So precision was key in my everyday work – lucky for me I am a stickler for perfection. In such a cutthroat industry in construction and property development, this further manifested deep within me my true driving force and purpose – to be a role model to my children. While others from my perspective may lose hope in humanity with constant dishonesty, deceit and greed, I use this to motivate and drive myself to stand out, to not diverge from the numerous lessons and values instilled deep within me, and always take pride in what I do.

I am blessed to have family and friends of the same mindset – both are loving and supportive to help me be the best version of myself. We support each other and build each other up to be proud of our achievements whether they are small or large. Overall, with the experience in numerous roles and the interaction with several inspirational figures, this has allowed me to create my own unique pathway granting me to be a better role model for my family and friends.

What is a challenge you have overcome?

Sometimes life has a funny way of teaching you lessons, mine came suddenly and with such pain to the point where I felt crippled by it. Loss of a parent, partner, husband, wife, child, friend or relative can be so unbearable.

My life as I knew it, complete with happiness and gratefulness, turned into complete despair and pain. On 8 November 2011 – 2 am, to be exact. It's the small things you remember in flashbacks – my husband answered the call. On his face was such a look of disbelief. As he looked at me and told me that my father had had a bad accident, I knew from the emotion on his face that it was serious – very serious. The reality was he had suffered a heart attack and had passed away. I lost all sense of reality at that moment. I honestly could not hear his voice – it felt as if I was in a dream and I would hopefully wake up soon.

Life as I knew it changed, my rock, my role model, my teacher had left our close-knit family, leaving my mother, brother and me and our families behind. There isn't a day that goes by where I don't think of him. I feel robbed of all the things he has missed and will miss in the future. What I would do just to share a moment with him – to have an espresso and laugh together. To think of the occasions he will miss, the graduations of my children and my nephews, the upcoming wedding of his only granddaughter, new homes, new projects, how proud he would be to see the successful business my brother has built.

It took a very long time to get to where I am now – being able to talk about him without tears welling in my eyes. Feelings of anger engulfed me for extended periods of time. My beautiful mother was grieving so my brother and I had to take care of everything. What happens is you are caught up with the mourning of a loved one, but business still runs in the background and you have to take care of both and care for everyone grieving. I was not dealing with it very well. I had two small children back then and I couldn't even pick them up from school because I couldn't control the grief. It is important to cherish all the moments with your loved ones, because we often take them for granted and never truly understand the past and imminent impact they have on you. This overwhelming feeling can never be removed, but it can be transformed and carried into something more meaningful to use as motivation when times are tough.

How did I overcome it? I took advice and went to see a grief counsellor. It was the best thing I did for myself. I felt embarrassed at first to even admit I needed the help but I just couldn't cope. I felt I was falling in a very dark deep hole. I needed someone to help me deal with the loss and move on, but be able to remember him and talk about him without the painful grief overwhelming me. It took a while but it was an important step in getting me back on track. I had thought I was invincible but no-one can truly walk down the sorrowful path of loss on their own. You need the help of family and friends to shape a new path of strength and unity. Sometimes you just have to put your hand up and say, *I am not okay and I need a little guidance.*

I am forever grateful for the support I had during such a difficult time. It's in these times of need you see the true meaning of love, support, courage and strength in people. Those are the ones you hold close to your heart.

What are your future plans?

I have always been the type of person that likes to plan everything ahead of time, so I am aware of the forthcoming hurdles that must be overcome and persevered. After my father passed away, my philosophy of life and planning changed.

I'm proud to say we have a few projects on the rise, including the building of our beautiful home, as well as upcoming events of celebration and reflection. Soon, I am hopeful and confident to manage and develop my own project, putting all I have learnt into reality. Going through this process, from consulting with numerous contractors to examining the final touches with the architect, will be both exhilarating and provide immense satisfaction.

Unfortunately, we are currently living through a pandemic, during which both of my children have completed their high school examinations, and so many businesses have closed – some of which may never reopen. These are testing times for one's mental health. We have to remember to be kind to ourselves, we must believe that these are minor setbacks, and we must continue to plan ahead. Even if the plan doesn't become a success, change it, but never change the goal. Thus, I have and will continue to plan our future investments as well as guide our children onto their pathways of success and happiness.

My hopes for the future are that we can move freely around and one day be able to travel overseas with my family to show my children their roots and heritage. Often my emotions become overrun with nostalgia – the familiar smells, the cuisine – it is an important part of me. My sincere hope is that my children may become grounded and successful in whatever avenue their heart desires and to grow with the foundation of knowledge and sacrifice laid down by my husband and me, and eventually one day take their father's business to new heights.

I plan and hope to continue in the construction and property development game together with my husband and children, an industry that I have grown to love and never tire of. In this ever-changing and volatile industry, one must adapt to it, and as a result successfully finance new projects and ventures. And with this comes new adventures, new challenges, ones we are ready to battle.

What advice would you give your thirteen-year-old self?

Find your passion, your drive, what you want to achieve in your life, and don't be fearful of any setbacks – think of it as life teaching you more lessons. Life happens, and we have to prepare for things to go wrong. It's what we take out of it that's important. It is vital to find a purpose, because often we may fall into an existential crisis or even become nihilistic, so it is pivotal we create meaning in our lives, as we are the only agents that have the responsibility to do so.

J K Rowling said it perfectly: 'Had I really succeeded at anything else, I might have never found the determination to succeed in the one arena I believe I truly belonged.'

Be prepared to come across people that will doubt you or your goals, this can sometimes bring your whole existence to a halt. Remain true to yourself, believe and trust your inner raging bull. With this perseverance and determination, it will drive your attitude to new levels and it will prove all those doubting you wrong. Success takes time, hard work and patience so I have learnt to enjoy the journey and remember to live in the moment. Learn to celebrate each milestone, no matter how significant, because these milestones reflect your hard work. Respect yourself and your decisions and the rest will follow you.

I look upon my parents' struggle in a new country, new language, new way of life, but it was determination and strength that drove them to achieve what they have now. Keeping true to themselves, building each other up each and every day, the unity and love they had for each other kept that dream of a brighter future and a successful life. My parents took nothing for granted and were grateful for every opportunity that came their way. But it was with pure unbreakable work ethic that drove them to achieve what they have today.

My late father used to say never forget where you came from, always try to remain grounded and humble.

Seek help if you feel you are struggling in any way and don't feel ashamed to ask for it, don't ever think lesser of yourself or allow anyone to treat you in this way. Be true to yourself as this is where the importance of family and friends come into hand, surround yourself with people who build you up and who immerse you in love and strength.

Despite offering these key pieces of advice to my younger self, I have no regrets, this is merely a reflection of where I have come, and often looking back allows one to develop and observe our perspectives and interactions, because without adaption often follows failure.

ABOUT NERINA LAHOUD

Life often goes by in a flash and one almost forgets their journey to the present moment. Through moments of happiness, sadness, tears, frustration, immense joy and piercing loss, you enter a reflective state in which you question how you got through it.

I am a mother of two wonderful teenage sons, and have worked full-time for twenty-five years with my husband in his property development/construction business, as the accounts office manager/PA. I feel privileged to have worked with such a brilliant man. I have learnt a considerable amount through this journey, not merely about business, but about all aspects of life. I am grateful to be able to experience each project with my husband, from design to construction and everything in-between. It is not always easy to work closely with someone that you live with, but with years of practise, I have been able to separate the two, as hard as it is at times.

From a young age, a robust work ethic was instilled in me, and as a result, I have always had high expectations of myself and take pride in my work and in the daily encounters with people I deal with. I am eternally thankful to be able to work my own hours so I could still be there for my sons – many times during their younger years I would bring them into the office to sleep while I worked late nights. These experiences have guided me to be appreciative of what you do, no matter how insignificant, to respect the people around you and always display compassion even if it is not reciprocated, and to also never burn your bridges – especially in business. People's memories of you always affect future encounters, thus, they remember how you treat them – whether good or bad. As long as you know the good you have done and when you get to a stage of channelling an altruistic outlook on life, you've truly become a role model to those around you. My heart is eternally engulfed in gratitude to be surrounded by a wonderful family and friends who I love and are precious to me.

But sometimes life has a funny way of teaching you lessons. Mine came suddenly and with such pain to the point I felt crippled by it. Loss of someone close to you does that. I used to hear my mother say to me to never take anything or anyone for granted. November 2011 was that turning point for me, where my life as I knew it to be – complete happiness and gratefulness – fell into complete devastation, despair and crippling grief. The phone call that happened at two in the morning, hearing my husband whispering only to be met by screams coming from the phone. How one day can craft a new outlook on life, and make you question all your decisions to that exact turning point. The man I looked up to that we all adored, the one that moulded the foundation for me to be a brave, successful and caring woman today, my father – was gone just like that.

It takes a loss of someone so close, that you love so much, to know how important a family-orientated life is.

PATRIZIA ANZELLOTTI

Curious | Tenacious | Daughter | Sister
Passionate about quality leaders.

Tell us your story to now

It's true that everyone has a story to tell, but for me, perhaps more important than the actual story itself, are the words I use to define myself that have created the person I am today. I am the eldest daughter in a migrant family, with great respect and gratitude for Australia and its opportunities. I am an observer, hard working, respectful of differences and appreciate the many excellent teachers I have known throughout my life.

My story really began when my father made the decision to take his chances and move to Australia. He was born and raised in Abruzzo, a rural region on the Adriatic Coast in Italy. The area had been devastated during WWII, and postwar, there was a great deal of poverty and very little opportunity. He was in his early twenties, and it must have been an incredibly brave decision for my parents to leave everything behind, family and friends in particular, to embark on a journey of discovery for a 'better life' in a new country where they didn't even speak the language.

I was born in Australia and my mother spoke very little English at the time. She tells the story of her dear friend who would visit her in the hospital every day after I was born to translate what the doctors were saying, so she was able to learn how to care for me. This continued when we went home. As she had very little support with all her family in Italy, her friends would come over and show her how to do things. My formative years were spent around my parents and the local community of friends they had made on their arrival to a new country. I was lucky to be surrounded by strong and capable, hard-working people who framed my life.

Growing up, my family had several small businesses and I have always been interested in the day-to-day working of business. I recognised early in life what good leadership can do for business and society. My parents worked hard, and my brother and I were given the greatest of opportunities; our parents sending us to the best schools they could afford.

My parents were very proud of their upbringing and their country of origin, and we were always an Italian family. The four of us were blessed to take trips to see our family in Italy and I was always excited to meet them, but I was also so pleased to come home to Australia.

From a young age, I was shown the value of hard work, and I've always been fortunate to have strong male and female role models in my life. I remember my first day of school where I spoke hardly any English and had to learn the language during my first few years of school. I was fortunate my parents were able to send me to a great school and I was encouraged and told that women can have a career as well as a family. You cannot become what you cannot see, and Australia had role models, teachers and people who helped me to develop my voice.

I was the first of my family, on both sides, to have a university education. My brother and I both completed double degrees and later took on the adventure of working in corporate Australia. University was new and different, with all sorts of people and experiences. It was here that I formed strong and lifelong friendships and really enjoyed learning and acquiring knowledge.

After completing an arts/law degree at the University of Sydney, I decided I did not want to practice law and moved into recruitment. When I first started work, diversity was not so apparent – Australia was male and Anglo-Saxon, but today, inclusivity has shifted and changed, as have the expectations of clients. Diversity and inclusion impacts the bottom line of organisations.

Today, I am a partner with Korn Ferry and work with global organisations that find and develop the world's best leaders. Today, and every day, I get to help organisations by finding and placing the best leaders on boards and executive teams in education, not-for-profit and government; areas that impact the quality and depth of our society.

We also work with organisations to build the strongest and most effective teams. In the last twelve months I've been very proud of some of the assignments I've led, including placing a woman as Australia's Chief Scientist, a First Nation's woman as the CEO of the NSW Law Society and the first female vice chancellor of the University of Wollongong.

Outside of work, I have had many passions in my life, but

the COVID-19 pandemic and the last eighteen months have taught me that good health, self-care, caring for your family and friends and being kind to the world around you are the most important things. I made peace with myself a long time ago that I would not have my own children, and embrace travel and contribution as my two strongest values.

My journey has held many wonderful experiences and often they include the value of learning from mistakes. If you can find a way to dust yourself off when something is broken you can move forward with resilience and strength. I can't stress this enough – mistakes allow us to see the contrast in the world, and if we can learn from them, we can truly grow.

I surround myself with open and honest people, with whom I can share the magical power of laughter.

What is your *why*?

I still remember the first time I heard my grandmother's story – I was very young, but it's a story that has stayed in my heart from that time.

It was the second world war and Abruzzo, where my family are from, was on the front line. My grandmother was pregnant with my aunt and my mother was just eighteen months old. The bombings were getting close to the village, and Grandfather and Grandmother acknowledged they would have to leave their home. My grandfather went up to the village the night before they were due to leave and never came back. My grandmother left the next morning, with no husband – his body was never found. She moved to the next region and following the birth of my aunt, when it was safe, returned to the village and began farming to survive. I often think of my grandmother's story and wonder how scared and sad she must have felt when her husband didn't come home. Despite her fears, she continued on her journey alone, pregnant and with a small child. She once told me that she did it for her children and future generations.

My mother also made a courageous journey of her own when she embarked on her move to Australia. I undoubtedly come from a line of strong, capable and resilient women who are prepared to make things happen.

Family is important to me and is the essence of my driving force, with my mother, father and brother still fortunate to be a very close-knit family – though sometimes we have to work at it!

Today, I am driven by supporting individuals and organisations to be the best they can be. Everyone should have the opportunity to grow, learn and prosper and I thrive on helping people find their leadership potential. I also enjoy helping organisations lift their leadership and performance. Gone are the days when corporations are just about making profit, and I love to see organisations flourish when they have a positive impact on humanitarian and environmental issues.

I'm sure it's not always commonly heard, but I love my job; I help organisations find the best person to lead them. I believe that good leadership in government, education and core purpose sectors make for a better society.

As an organisation, at Korn Ferry, we change people's lives.

What is a challenge you have overcome?

It may seem unusual for a woman in my position, but self-confidence is not my thing! It is a challenge that I acknowledge, work with and push through every day. I believe my resilience and self-belief in my professional skills help me with this challenge.

Most recently, I have seen many challenges, both professional and personal, over the last two years of living through the COVID-19 pandemic. This time has shown me how fragile the outside world can be without strong and capable leaders. I have learnt the importance of resilience, courage and focus.

A challenge for my parents, more than myself because I was so young, was that I was born with some medical eye issues. It was a small thing for me as I did not understand it, but when I was first born, my parents were told I would need a few operations. In a new country and with very basic English it was difficult to understand what their new baby would have to go through. When they tell the story now, they talk about the wonderful doctors and friends who stood beside them to help them make the decision; the friends who stayed with them in the hospital during my operations, and the ones who came to see me every day and help with the rehabilitation.

I have very few memories of this time but I am incredibly grateful to have good sight, not only for the obvious reasons, but because I have a love of art and have been to wonderful galleries all over the world to see amazing works.

What are your future plans?

My main focus for the future is to ensure I do all I can to encourage diversity and inclusion of all people in our country. Over the last two years, the organisation I work for has had the opportunity to closely look at our vision and values, and I feel fortunate that we are all focused on a common goal; to give everyone the opportunity to reach their full potential. I believe this will create a strong and inclusive world that will enhance society on so many levels.

My personal plans are not too complex. I intend to continue on focusing on the importance of self-care, as well as supporting family and friends in any way I can. I will do my best to ensure that I do no more harm to the environment and leave it as a better place for generations to come. Professionally, I hope to continue to practice in all ways that I can, to help grow and foster the potential in people.

The future is about ensuring that I live by these values.

What advice would you give women starting in business?

Take a leap of faith …

I have always admired the brave and strong women who have the courage to start their own businesses. It's not for the faint-hearted, but taking a leap into working for yourself can bring amazing rewards. I have the following advice:

- Don't doubt yourself – if you have an idea and you're passionate about it, go for it!
- Connect with people who have done it before. It's so helpful to have a network of people who can share their experiences.
- Know the people in your team who will give you frank and fearless advice, even if it's not what you want to hear.
- Learn how to read the numbers and what questions to ask. Make sure you know the bottom line for your business, how many sales it takes to make a profit, and exactly what your ROI is.

- Know what you are famous for and understand your business' uniqueness. Your strengths will set you apart from your competition.
- Hire smart people who hold your organisation's values and act them out with your customers.
- Create a culture where ideas are wanted, appreciated and listened to. Value your employee's input.
- Work hard but pause, recharge and restart. It's so important to have some balance and self-care.
- Know yourself, what you are good at and what support you need to build a successful business. Understanding the areas in business where you need help will support you to build an awesome team.
- Understand your supply chain and know how they work. Never rely too heavily on one option – always have a backup.
- You don't have all the answers – know where to get them. Understanding and accepting there are things you just don't know will be invaluable in your growth.
- Know and care for your customers. Your business is there to serve your customers' needs, so be sure to make decisions with the customer in mind.
- Don't overthink things. Sometimes we can think about decisions for way too long!
- Say thank you and sorry when needed. Nobody is perfect, so being able to say sorry if you make a mistake is imperative to good relationships. Likewise, saying 'thank you' shows you appreciate it when someone does a good job or helps you in some way.
- Know your competitors. There is always someone else

providing a similar service or product to your ideal customer.

- Know your elevator pitch – you will need it often.
- Just when you are sick of hearing something is when you just start to hear the message.
- Ask the right questions. Learn how to ask questions that will give you the answers you need.
- Deal with issues quickly. If you procrastinate for too long, small issues can become big issues.
- Laugh, have fun and celebrate wins – even the small ones. (I can't stress this highly enough!)
- Trust your inner voice. Often, it's the voice you first hear when a decision needs to be made that will work out best for you!

'Never doubt that a small group of thoughtful, committed citizens can change the world. Indeed, it is the only thing that ever has.' – Margaret Mead

ABOUT PATRIZIA ANZELLOTTI

My story really began by a decision taken by my father when he was in his early twenties in postwar Italy. We are from Abruzzo, a rural region that was a front line in World War II. There was very little opportunity there so he decided to come to Australia. It is here that my brother and I were given the greatest of opportunities – my parents sent us to the best schools they could afford. I was then the first in my family on both sides to get a university education.

Growing up, I was shown the value of hard work and contribution to a country that was so very accepting and filled with opportunity. I have always been fortunate to have strong role models – male and female.

My family have a small business and it is from seeing this that the workings of business has always interested me. I also recognised early in life what good leadership can do for business and society. After compleing an arts/law degree at the University of Sydney I realised I did not want to practice law. I moved into recruitment and am now a partner with Korn Ferry and global human capital organisations that finds and develops the best leaders. We also work with orgnisations to build the strongest and most effective teams. In the last twelve months I have been very proud of some of the assignments that I have led placing a woman as Australia's Chief Scientist, First Nation's woman as the CEO of the NSW Law Society and the first female vice chancellor of the University of Wollongong.

The journey has had many experiences that include the value

of learning from mistakes, surrounding yourself with people to who are open and honest, listening and knowing that mistakes can be fixed, finding ways to dust yourself off when you have broken something and the magical power of laughter.

AMREETA ABBOTT

Entrepreneur | Leader | Innovator
Visionary & Traveller

Tell us your story to now

In his speech, after being awarded the 1995 Nobel Prize for Literature in Stockholm, the famed Irish poet Seamus Heaney defined a way of living your life that I think every girl and woman can take as good advice. Sometimes, he said, you have to, 'Walk on air against your better judgement.'

For much of my career I've done that. To go where no-one had gone before. In a world of accelerating technology, I found a way to harness that and put it to use – on behalf of anyone seeking strategic advantage by making it easier to conduct business or live life.

Heaney certainly embodied that concept. When he died, it made the front page of newspapers around the world. And when an entire football stadium heard the news over the announcement system they stood as one and clapped for two full minutes.

No football stadium will stand in tribute for me, and that's not a problem. Still, I like, in idle moments, to think that female entrepreneurs should expect that kind of attention for what we, as a growing group, contribute to society worldwide. We often approach things in different ways – and that's good. We see things from a different angle – and that is also good.

We are practical, driven, persistent in our drive and desire to not only get it right but to excel. To lead. Do good. Be smart. Change society. Make it better for us having been involved.

In many ways – and not defining it as anything other than teenage angst – that was how I felt growing up in a small Victorian country town. But I was getting good grades at school, particularly maths, even though it wasn't my favourite subject. So, over the years, and particularly in my later teens, I came to realise this town and the 5,000 people who lived in it – through no fault of their own – couldn't deliver on what I wanted from my life. I couldn't define then exactly what I wanted; I just knew I had to get out of there to achieve that.

To get the best start I researched different types of loans, negative gearing, financial techniques and instruments, basic economics and accounting. I'd gravitated towards finances very early on. My father wanted me to have a much better education than he had, and the first book he gave me was *Think and Grow Rich* by Napoleon Hill. Others followed about stocks and shares.

Looking back, my approach was logical and practical from the start.

Recognising I needed to work, learn how to budget and take care of myself financially, I went to a financial adviser. To his absolute astonishment I demonstrated I already knew a lot about the basics. He offered me a job, declaring I'd learned more about money and finance than some of the people in his office. And so, I started!

I moved through the financial services industry, absorbing everything I could about products and how the systems around them worked. Or didn't. That led me to focus more on technology and the appreciation of what it could do. One day I realised I was a fintech. I still am. To this day, entirely focused on areas ripe for digital transformation.

From the moment I bought my first house, I realised how unnecessarily complicated signing documents was. My background was already filled with accounting, SMSFs and financial advice, and I was developing a deep understanding of the finance industry. But I was getting perplexed over what I now call the *friction points* of business transactions.

The businesses I started were dedicated to solving these. I'll tell any young woman to read widely and deeply. I still don't have a TV at home. I do stream a lot, but I convinced myself broadcast television would distract me. And once I started, I had to keep going because I had staff, casual workers and clients to take care of by then.

The concepts that created NowInfinity were taking shape piece by piece in my head. It's like a dream you have where the answer is just out of reach, and then with one precise moment, you have it. It hit me. People weren't getting documents when they needed them. Their dreams were being delayed because documents weren't being delivered for signature. They'd spend days of their time chasing and then delivering them to companies.

And to companies which then had to find the space to file all that paper away correctly because the documents would probably be needed again and again. They had to pay rent for the premises in which the paper was stored and pay staff to do all the work. In fact, it was an endless paper chain. Nothing efficient about that. But there was a way to correct it. Change everything. NowInfinity was born that day.

A whole series of things I'd read coalesced into the knowledge that outsourcing overseas was the way for someone like me to start my own business; it was essential to get my costs under control. I went to the Philippines. I met some people there who've been with me for years now – I wouldn't change any of them for the world, and they are real friends and not just colleagues.

That's the case with Vitalii, my trusty chief technical officer and great friend. Today, a decade and a half on, he's one of the key people in my new ventures. We continue to develop business together. He is one of the country's leading experts in so many technical fields.

So as a busy young woman in Australia, I had teams in the Philippines, I had a team in Ukraine and in Australia. Outsourcing has its ups and downs, but I had chosen well. I visited and found them engaging. We'd used technology to find each other and I backed that up face to face. Anyone starting today can do the same, and the choices for communicating are so much better.

In retrospect, it was essential that we initially sit down and talk things through. The key to teamwork is where individuals start to shine, and become committed to each other and the overall plan of the business. It wasn't something I had to force: my team members quickly not only displayed their already outstanding talent and remarkable determination but an understanding that if we were to go where few had gone before in terms of our technology, each of them had to push themselves further.

To see them do that and to share the pleasure they got when they were able to do it was both humbling and a delight. It encouraged me as a leader to push myself even further; in some ways, we'd become a self-perpetuating unit. Stones being polished into diamonds. I was proud of where we were going.

We seemed to overcome what used to be the tyranny of distance easily. Technology and communication advances made the job seamless.

Growing a business involves more than hard work. It involves emotion, pushing past exhaustion, getting through one way or the other. In the end, it all works.

Eight years down the track, I'd grown my business NowInfinity to the point where it could be sold. We disrupted the legal, accounting and financial services industries through technology. We allowed accounting professionals, for instance, to create and manage outcomes for their clients by offering every document needed for the client business digitally.

Open collaboration is not only the key – it is the future. Consumers expect it, and business also does. And people in my industry learned a lesson I learned very early on and will never let go – they expect fintechs to care about their bottom line.

As CEO it was my job to focus on innovation relentlessly. Today, create the best way in the world to do something. Tomorrow, improve on that. And keep going.

I'd made a very conscious decision, way back at the very start, not to review in detail a competing market product. I recognised them all, of course, but some instinct kicked in to tell me, *If you know in detail what they do, you'll settle to do the same.* I didn't want to go down that path. Leading may be lonely but far better than following.

There are a few moments more seriously rewarding than when an accounting practice or a business organisation tells you how much they value what you've done and how they have been able to improve what they do at all levels by using your product and technology. It instantly creates a feeling of joy and gratitude at the privilege of being able to help them experience that. To introduce substantial cost savings and efficiencies into their operations.

More than once I've sat back and counted the number of developers I had in comparison to the remaining staff and that was the surreal moment where I thought, *I own a fintech company,* as I remembered how I started with so little and recognised where determination and applied technical creativity had taken me.

Early in 2020, we were able to sell NowInfinity to an ASX-listed company Class Limited for $25 million. I'll talk later about the emotions involved in that, but there was one immediate one.

It challenged me to come up with something entirely new. A whole new energy, to not sit back and relax on laurels but drive me to build the next big thing.

My business has always been about digital transformation, streamlining workflows by making manual processes electronic, reducing complex processes into something much more manageable, and saving any business time and money, and becoming more efficient and productive. It allows them to grow.

We all realised, I think during COVID-19, we no longer

actually needed to go into banks, accountants' offices or even shops. It kept people safe and it kept businesses afloat. We could do it all digitally. And it didn't need to be complicated.

Even more than that, it is now the way forward globally in our post-pandemic world.

As we developed NowInfinity, I'd realised how partnering with a global multinational improved not only my business but also benefitted them.

So, with a whole new world to conquer with NowInfinity now owned by someone else, I created several other companies, the main one being Annature, a business based on richly featured e-signing, ISO certified and affordable. My team and I have already improved the concept of electronic signatures. We are the first certified premium solution in the market.

It fits what Spanx founder Sara Blakely once said, 'Don't be intimidated by what you don't know. That can be your greatest strength and ensure that you do things differently from everyone else.'

In this case, we did know something. We'd been in this area of business before, but it was ripe for some Australian innovation. That has given us a powerful advantage. The world has changed. It is an opportunity for all of us to expand our boundaries.

I'm as excited about that as I was the day I first started. It'll develop with vision and smart partner integrations. It's already attracted attention and direct involvement from Qantas, one of the world's biggest and most astute and admirable corporations.

I have a team. Clients. Challenges. And a reason to get up in the morning. Every day is new. I couldn't be happier.

What is your *why*?

If I could stop thinking, I would. And if I did that, I'd stop working. And where would the fun be in that?

Creative thinking about business was something I developed early. The need to use technology for improvement, to open up possibilities that didn't and couldn't exist decades ago, but possibilities we as a team could create, to push a venture even further.

Game isn't the correct word and *vocation* is maybe too strong but a nonstop mission to hammer against and through what had been accepted boundaries and make them disappear.

I have a journalist friend who says journalism is a poor person's way to be part of history. Fintech is the same. I thrive on business challenges, streamlining, seeing connections not immediately apparent to others and then making the change happen. What we do, and I think this should attract more women into our industry, is show them how to change the world – and the way the world interacts. In a sense, you're making history.

I'm attracted by the notion that if I think of doing something in a practical way we can put it to use for a client. A different way of conducting their business maybe; a different way of cooperating with their customers, easing the burden every day.

Not everyone is lucky enough to be able to work in an industry the way they want. To feel or know they are adding value. Sometimes you have to go and find the industry; in my case, it seemed to have found me.

We'd created a juggernaut with NowInfinity, by allowing people to overcome the frustrations of filling out ASIC forms, setting up companies, trusts and SMSFs and so much more.

As the leader of the company, I found myself being forced

more and more away from what I do best – generating ideas and generating ideas fast for the companies we serve. When you have forty or fifty staff, they become the daily focus and you find yourself becoming more involved in the daily transactions of the company. Besides, we'd grown magnificently and other, bigger, companies could see the value we'd created in ourselves by creating value for hundreds of other businesses.

Inevitably the decision had to be made. The company was big enough and profitable enough for a very successful sale. So, we did that.

Then something remarkable happened. It allowed me to become *me* again. Failure has never been an option. We've all had failures in our lives and in our professions but regard things like that as learning, and being agile, and then move on. It doesn't mean it doesn't hurt sometimes, but there are so many things in our lives that can be improved that it can be easier to move along and fix the things you can fix better than most.

COVID-19 has cramped much of the world. It sent our axes spinning off-centre, on a tilt that, for a time, looked like it could become permanent. Not anymore. The world is fighting back.

My driving force is finding an outlet for the tempest of ideas struggling for both space and expression in my head. Many, I know, have to subdue that kind of thought process. I'm keen to encourage others to go with it. That's how the world advances.

One of the many things that motivated me before air travel was restricted was the capacity just to fly away. Literally. Golf was never for me. I'm telling you this only because I want to encourage young and not-so-young women entrepreneurs and would-be entrepreneurs to do something similar. Something that allows you time to think. Mine was to get on a plane and take off to Thailand, for instance. Get to the airport in Bangkok, freshen up, get back on the plane again and fly back to Australia.

Rationale? There was no competing noise or demands on my attention – all those hours in the air. I was cosseted, pampered, able to put on headphones and either watch a movie or just zone. Let the ideas in my head insist on being heard. So that at the end of a weekend up in the air, they had rearranged themselves. I developed some focus. The real ones got to the top. I was relaxed. My business was the beneficiary, and the improved concept that flowed from that benefitted one or scores of other businesses. Benefitted people. There's no bigger bonus than that.

What is a challenge you have overcome?

We can all feel intimidated from time to time by work, life, self-doubt and fear. It would be unnatural not to. But these are things that can sabotage your progress or crash your potential as a business owner and leader.

I encountered one after selling the company.

The last thing I'd expected was that it would have been so emotional letting it go. Nothing could have prepared me for that. It was a genuine emotional shock. The build-up years had been intense and personally rewarding. The days, weeks and months of doing things and either luck or chance or brilliant teamwork or good judgment producing a good result. We all understand, at some core level, that if you do something you love long enough and consistently enough and with everything else being equal, you rise to the top – and that is recognised everywhere.

In accounting practice, I'd set up companies and trusts. At NowInfinity, we were producing 5,000 documents a day. I'd been dealing with ASIC over the precise legal and accounting detail we needed to factor into what we produced for clients so they didn't run afoul of the regulator. All of this was absorbing work and became a way of life – continuous, setting new standards, always looking for ways to develop and move forward.

Suddenly, it was gone – no email address. No office. No team to talk to. There must be a survival gene for entrepreneurs or people who won't stop after one success to bask in a glory that is no longer theirs. Mine kicked into action again, and suddenly, starting over gave me the most energetic boost I'd had in years.

Technology changes every aspect of our lives. I read recently about a company that developed a 3D printer for the military and used it to print metal parts for rugged army vehicles 1,200 km from any service point. Seeing advances like that in other fields encourages me to work out similar advances we can introduce into ours.

As you can see, I've always been self-motivated. The challenges any entrepreneur faces are keeping the focus on customers, using technology to ensure operations improve at every level, overseeing finance and transactions, evaluating risk as a manager and being people-centric.

Executing those skills well is the journey, being enthusiastic about it has never been a problem. Being the leader of the pack means you not only have to keep an eye on everything that is happening in the present, but you also have to maintain a vision for the future. Not least because every team member looks to you for decisions on which everyone's future depends.

I always loved the line, 'Get busy living or get busy dying,' from the movie *The Shawshank Redemption*. Not just because it was first written by Stephen King in the novel on which the movie is based but because the line is first said by the character Andy Dufresne played by Tim Robbins, and then repeated by 'Red' Redding played by Morgan Freeman.

It plays into another theme of that great movie: hope. So, while challenges may seem fearsome at the time, you've got a choice: throw your hands in the air and give up or get proactive and get moving on your terms.

There's no choice, is there?

Getting busy means you'll leave your imprint on the world, small or large.

What advice would you give your thirteen-year-old self?

Not just in boardrooms, but across the executive leadership teams of ASX-listed companies in Australia, only a quarter are women. I know that when I started out running the business, I was more than once referred to as 'the secretary'.

Things have improved from then, but there's a way to go. Google is alive with advice links to young women, everywhere from Disney (princess theory) to the UN (global empowerment, but it's a big world).

I have more considerable confidence in young women. And my advice is very straightforward: work it out, go for it and let nothing stand in your way. If you can't break through an obstacle – human or otherwise – go around it. And keep going.

There are reams of lists on the web and shelves full of business books about the key points to keep in mind to have some chance of success. My personal top ten:

1. Mentorship is the first step. I've been blessed by having one or two mentors in my life who were trusted advisers. Their input was invaluable.

2. Dream big. If you have an idea, even if it is a bit fuzzy at times, set it as a goal. That's the first step towards making it happen.

3. Networking is the most significant source of ideas you might ever experience. It can also be the most energising thing you do. My last trip was to New York, introducing our first API bot, 'Rosie', to the market.

4. Know who you are. And by extension, what you want. Take some time to understand and be honest about your ambitions. You don't need always to share them, but you do need to know what they are.

5. Collaboration makes the world go around. You don't need to be in conflict. That will slow you down, and in extreme situations, divert you from your goal. That doesn't mean you cave in to pressure – ignore it and move forward.

6. Talented and skilled people on your teams and in your business are everything. The ones who are indeed champions of you and what you do make themselves known. Cherish them – it could begin a lifelong friendship, professional and personal.

7. Take responsibility. It's on you.

8. Intuition is never wrong, even when your conscious mind screams, *Just take the safe way!* If something feels wrong, it is. So, fix it.

9. Be nimble. Agile. If your perspective or approach is open to

changing yourself, use your professional advice in light of facts and your insights.

10. I've mentioned already putting aside time to think – moments of stillness. Mine sometimes was and will be a little extreme, but you can lock the door, sit down and let your brain cool down. Works wonders.

There is a common thread in people who develop successful companies – they approach problem-solving from all sides. Taking the often-exceptional solution their team has come up with and applying the entrepreneurial mindset. Often that involves thinking differently than the rest. Once you realise you can do that, you can deepen that way of thinking even further.

It becomes a reflex and a habit because you know and you've learned that your first solution may not be the best one. And you recognise when you have the correct answer.

Becoming an entrepreneur or a top executive is potentially one of the most challenging paths for any woman. Take heart. It is not at all impossible, and the odds are slowly moving in our direction.

In Australia, about 38% of small businesses are owned by women, and that will continue to grow. In the ten years up to 2019, women accounted for two-thirds of the 170,000 newly established businesses.

Many of these were small. We all started small. Even the hardships caused by the pandemic infused us with something else: more agility, more courage, more ability to see beyond what we were doing in business terms – and finding ways to surmount often great difficulties.

Go for it. Your mindset will change your own world first, those around you and eventually the world at large. It is the most exhilarating experience. We need women in leadership roles. We need more women with more financial independence.

The first step is the vision to succeed and succeed big, and reading this book is a clear sign you have that vision.

At the beginning of this chapter, I mentioned a quote from the Nobel Laureate poet Seamus Heaney. It's worth closing it with something else he wrote. It's now also painted on a gable wall in Dublin.

Just minutes before he died, he texted his wife with a short message. In Latin, two words: *noli timere* – don't be afraid.

Advice for any woman, anywhere.

Good luck to you.

ABOUT AMREETA ABBOTT

Imagine living in a world where you're told you're not good enough, where you don't belong and you shouldn't even bother. This is the world I saw and experienced over the years as a woman in business. It is from this place that I have tried to change the narrative. Life can really suck, let me tell you. You start a business with the person you trust and love, only to be screwed over and left trying to bring the pieces together, and still increase results tenfold every year, because that's what we do as women. We grind, we hustle, we thrive – we're raising children and growing economies at the same time.

My name's Amreeta Abbott and I started my first business with my now ex-husband in 2012, and in 2020, I sold – that's right, 'I' sold – it for $25 million, bootstrapped with no capital investment, no husband, just a s$%t ton of passion and energy. At the time, I didn't have all the answers when it came to building the business, but f$%k, have I made a load of mistakes – not failures, but mistakes – that I can help you avoid.

I'm a proud mum of two boys and call the Gold Coast my home. My heart is to see businesses succeed and expand. I invest my time, sweat and tears into technology that relieves pain points with an industry making the experience of doing business better. Not just a little better, I mean f$%king great!

Less than 1% of startup businesses ever achieve the entrepreneur's dream of a multimillion-dollar sale, but that's what I did. The number of female-led technology startups to have achieved this feat you could count on one hand! You and I are both here to help each other change this narrative. There needs to be more female-led founders changing the world, and I want to help! We are Global Girls and we're in this together. Grab your girls, start a book club and join the movement!

KAREN McDERMOTT

Publisher | Author | Mentor | Mother
Passionate about sharing stories with the world.

Tell us your story to now

I could write many books on the stories that I have to share in my lifetime, but from a global girls' perspective which is united, connected and forward moving, I'd like to share my story to now from where I grew up with a curious, excited, adventurous aspect and perspective of life. I was excited by life, by the potential of it. I never knew exactly what I wanted to do or be, but I embraced the essence of life as if it was this magical gift, and I couldn't understand why others didn't feel the same way. My enthusiasm for life – I think it just glowed from me.

I was always told that when I entered a room I glowed, but I realise that it was only when I was surrounded by people that were *my* people. And that's what school was for me.

We had moved from the Republic of Ireland to Northern Ireland when I was nine years old. It was a totally different education system. I had no friends even though the distance was only six miles across the border between the schools I attended. It could have been the other end of the world, it was such a different experience. But I just went, got on with it and did what I could. I looked out for my sisters who were also at the school.

Then I transitioned to secondary school, where I was an A student and where I felt I truly belonged. There was a recall of the eleven-plus qualifying exam to get into prestigious schools. My results were some of the results that were reassessed and it was said that I passed the exam! And so, at age eleven, I was offered a place at a prestigious all-girls convent grammar school. Well, my parents' eyes lit up and they were just so proud.

I couldn't say no. But I was happy where I was and so it was one of those sliding-door moments. Was I better off staying at the secondary school where I was top of the class, where I felt I belonged, where I shined? Or was I better going to the convent grammar school that had the prestige but that I never felt connected or enthusiastic about learning in? It's an interesting predicament and I know it was a big catalyst in my life.

Convent grammar school life was interesting for the first three years. I just went through the motions, I never engaged in class as the teaching style was not something I connected with, I was bored all the time, and apart from one time in Maths when Mr Martin asked us a brainteaser that no-one in the class got except me, I realised that I was a total out-of-the-box thinker and that wasn't encouraged in a convent grammar school.

And so for the last two years I ended up getting involved with some of the cool girls (and yes, started smoking). In school, I just focused on what I did best which was being curious and having fun and starting to feel alive again. But it wasn't through the teacher that I was being taught. It was through the connections with my friends and the experiences we had doing the 'wrong' things like skipping school. But I could not wait to leave school and went straight into work.

I worked in a tights factory checking tights for ladders, would you believe, at sixteen years old? But I loved it. It was fun. We were all working around a table, having fun together. I was the youngest, but I wasn't there very long when I got offered a job in a local factory closer to home which I had the deepest sense of belonging to.

It was a community. But I naturally always ended up being the boss because I had leadership qualities and I loved being there. I was a supervisor for many years, which was a very secure income.

But then I had my son. I was a single mum and so I had to take him to my mother for her to look after while I worked. We were in Ireland, and when it was very cold or I was on late shift having to pick him up from his Grandmother's at 10 pm, it just didn't feel right – it didn't align with my values.

So, I ended up leaving work and went back to school. I studied humanities, which I loved. Then I went on to work three part-time jobs as well. Around that time, I met and ended up falling in love with my now-husband and we had my second son.

When he was five months old my whole life imploded and I fell into PTSD after an incident happened in my home. It was a very dark period, but I call it my cocoon period because I did a lot of inner work during that time. One thing I do know is that the reason I fell into PTSD was because I was running on empty, I was pouring into everyone else but not myself and so the inevitable happened.

When I finally came out of that period – which was through the wake-up call of a double miscarriage – I started to feel again, I started to get excited by life again. I had this not-caring-what-anybody-else-thought attitude because we all only live once, we have one life to experience and I never wanted to feel the deadness inside that comes with post-traumatic stress. So, with curiosity and love in my heart, I started saying yes to things. And so when our visa came that year to come to Australia, we just didn't even think about it. We just came.

New life, new start, new beginnings. It was really tough at the beginning because it was one of those times when there were a lot of people depending on me and I was in a new culture. We came to Australia when I was thirty-five weeks pregnant with my daughter and we knew nobody, but we built a life around that and it's one of those things that I will never regret because it ended up being best thing in my life. That happened because I found writing, and then publishing, and that has been an absolute joy.

Despite this, my heart never had the answer it longed for, which was why did I have a double miscarriage?

Why did I lose those babies that I wanted so much? The miscarriage took two weeks and it was a long process. But then I had my epiphany, and subsequently I ended up writing my first novel in 2010 in one month during NaNoWriMo, which was just the most amazing experience. It not only healed me from the inside because of the therapeutic effect of writing my story entwined into a novel, it was so emotionally and spiritually freeing.

But when my stories ended up getting published and found

their way into the hearts and minds of those who needed to read them and they made a difference, well, that just fuelled my fire for story and how story can change someone else's life. When you take time and have the courage to share it, when it resonates with someone, it heals or it ignites something within them that nothing else can. So since 2010, I have been on an absolute crusade to help stories get told, and what an adventure has it brought me on! I've had so many amazing experiences, so many wonderful things have happened to me and so many wonderful people have connected with me, I've won so many wonderful awards and just lived my dream life. But, all whilst having my six kids, I was able to be that hands-on mum. And yes, I'm human, I get distracted by things, but ultimately I'm here always for my kids.

To do life on my own terms is a huge privilege. I want others to realise that when you really connect with yourself, connect with your values and work through those with your dreams, they really can come true – it's amazing how the universe provides what we need to make it all happen.

So right now, it's January 2022. I'm forty-four years old. I have a huge year ahead of me. There's a film in the mix, there's a lot of publishing, yes, but also a lot of writing, a lot of my books are being published this year and there's some huge things happening and I'm so excited, by the way, that my life has gone on this beautiful tangent and this beautiful momentum and it's making a difference for others and it's helping stories get shared. And I'm helping people embrace and value the magic in life and awaken to their potential possibilities.

You don't need to be asleep in life. My goodness, I look at

what I've experienced over my forty-four years – I've experienced so much! And yes, it may frighten others to go ahead and do some of the things that I've done, but when you know, you know, and I'm very connected to my knowing. So, I never fear the unknown, because I have true faith that it is leading me to my destiny, to what I set intentions for energetically, because that's what the universe does. It aligns with what you put out there energetically and delivers what it is that you want.

And we need only ask what we want. So moving forward, I will be sharing stories, yes, but I will also be walking with others to really realise their true potential and what they can manifest out of their lifetime. Because too many dreams are going unfulfilled, too many lives are just staying stagnant. And we need more good people out there realising their dreams, putting themselves first, because then we can show up as the best version of ourselves and pour into others. And that ripple effect in the world will make the world that we live in a better place, will make the population happier people because they will be fulfilled, they will have made the difference in their life and that will ripple along to everyone around them, their families and communities.

Because once you touch the life of one person, that ripples out and touches the lives of all of the people around them. And that is a beautiful tsunami of love throughout the world. That's the kind of thing that we need happening. And then we can watch our world heal, not only through people healing, but natural healing, because the energy will be around to have it. Nourished – because I'm never going to give up on the fact that love makes the world go on.

Love is what helps things to flourish. And when we embrace it and value love more, we see what happens in our world. And just remember that love is ten times stronger than any hurt. So, it only takes one person to eradicate ten people's hurts, but we can't give up on them. Everyone deserves the opportunity to choose the goodness in their lives for themselves. It's up to them.

My story to now has been an adventure. I'm excited about the future and I have had more experiences in my forty-four years than a lot of people have had in two lifetimes. I'm very blessed.

I am a mum of six children aged from six to twenty-five. I have given two TedX talks to date and another one this year. I write for *Forbes*. I've written over forty books, I have helped over four hundred authors get published and I feel so privileged to have made the impact I have in the world. And I will continue to do so always.

And I will go with the ebbs and flows of where I need to be and where I'm called to be, because that's what we need to do – show up and make that difference.

What is your *why*?

My driving force is the impact that stories can have on the world. I have personal and also humanitarian motivation behind what I do. I got to create a business that allowed me to have financial freedom whilst having the work-life balance that I wanted. That was my perfect balance for me so that I could still be a present mum. To show up for my dreams and desires and then also the power of story, how it connects with people, heals people, ignites things within people.

Joining authors on their journey to share their stories is a huge privilege. It's an honour to be there from the start to the finish. And there's never a finish when it comes to a book, there's always more that can be done. But to go on that journey of those words, going out into the world and reaching people through books, through audiobooks, through interviews. All of these things is when you see me showing up because they connect people in a good way.

Even if it erupts something within someone, it means that the progression is happening. They get to release something that may be holding them down, to explore and grow through something. So words are important and we need to be mindful of just how important they are, just how powerful they are. And that is a true driving force for me.

The second part of my driving force is because I pursued something I was very passionate about and became very successful around it.

Whilst not compromising any of my values, I'm absolutely driven to share my seven life principles with the world because we share how we find solutions to things that work for us. It's our duty to share that with the world so that other people can learn from that and find their own way. So, it's not that we find ways to do things and just lock them in our bank. We need to share with others so they can learn from that. They can make choices with that and be inspired and maybe incorporate some of what we learn that works for us into their lives too.

What is a challenge you have overcome?

Firstly, I'd like to share my perspective on challenges. In my lifetime, I've discovered my perspective on challenges has changed, especially when I became a non-profit. Challenges are a part of any journey, and so how we look at them and how we approach them is very important. Each challenge is an opportunity to pause, to learn something new or to let something go.

So, if it's learning something new, it's an opportunity to stop and grow into the person we need to be to get those things that we set intentions for. If we pause and stop and don't go any further with that pursuit, it's because it's taken from us and we must reassess and realise it's not worth it for us. Some people push through at that point, and they just keep facing challenge upon challenge upon challenge that they never feel fulfilled with. But the right challenges are there to help you grow into the person that you need to be, and achieving your goals is just the very next step.

It's a beautiful process. Nothing is ever going to be just handed to you. The journey is one that it is a quest, it is an adventure, and when you pursue it with curiosity, it's amazing how much more fun the journey is. And your perspective of challenges changes. I get excited when a challenge comes before me because I know I'm growing.

I know that I'm going through a stage of growth and evolution, and that's part of who I am. It's part of what I choose to embrace.

What are your future plans?

I'm here talking to you now at the beginning of 2022.

It's my tenth year with Serenity Press, which is wonderful. I've learned a lot. I've grown a lot, and we have a lot more to do.

2022 is also my life number alignment year because twenty-two is my number. I live in number twenty-two. I'm age forty-four, which is double twenty-two.

I'm focused a lot on my authorship this year. We'll see how things go. It's exciting to think of what can happen with where I'm going this year with my seven life principals, my teachings, and it's my driving force to help others see the potential of their lives and realise what they can achieve. So, we're going to be building out my Life Magic Alchemy series. I'm very excited to see where that goes and to just show up and talk about how you can be the best version of yourself just by the power of your thoughts. It's the most beautiful thing.

So, my plan is lots of books, lots of opportunities to share my thoughts and my principles with everyone and growth.

What advice would you give your thirteen-year-old self?

The key piece of advice I would give to my thirteen-year-old self is to just keep being you. I was pretty happy when I was thirteen. Although I wasn't a great lover of school, I had a curious sense of adventure about life. I didn't know where I was going, I didn't know what I wanted to be, but I didn't have any anxiety about not knowing any of that.

I just got on with doing things – and I was the eldest of six, so I had a lot of family stuff to do. I had some good friendships that I still have today. I was very blessed, I had loving parents. Life was good.

So I would tell my thirteen-year-old self that there's going to be bumpy rides.

There's going to be times when some things are tougher

than others. But to just keep that curious sense of adventure and allow yourself to live through that and always choose the positive rather than the negative. Because you can't have a positive and a negative thought at the same time.

ABOUT KAREN McDERMOTT

Karen is an award-winning publisher, author, TEDx speaker and advanced law of attraction practitioner.

Author of numerous books across many genres – fiction, motivational, children's and journals – she chooses to lead the way in her authorship generously sharing her philosophies through her writing.

Karen is also a sought-after speaker who shares her knowledge and wisdom on building publishing empires, establishing yourself as a successful author-publisher and book writing.

Having built a highly successful publishing business from scratch, signing major authors, writing over thirty books herself and establishing her own credible brand in the market, Karen has developed strategies and techniques based on tapping into the power of knowing to create your dreams.

Karen is a gifted teacher who inspires others to make magic happen in their lives through her seven life principles that have been integral in her success.

When time and circumstance align, magic happens.

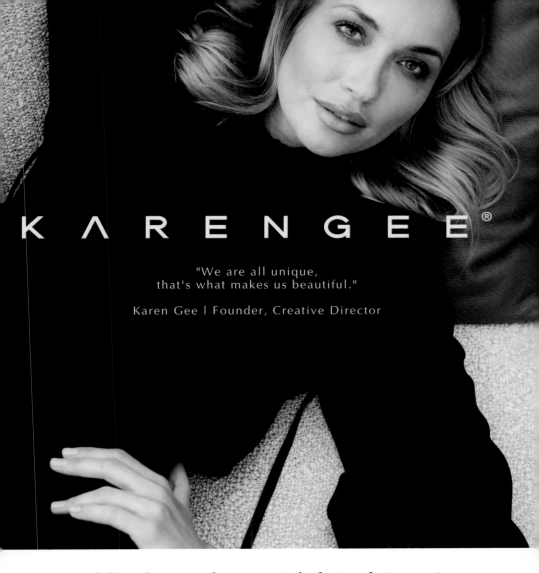

KARENGEE®

"We are all unique,
that's what makes us beautiful."

Karen Gee | Founder, Creative Director

Our philosophy is simple – exquisitely designed pieces using quality fabric. We put a lot of thought into our designs, from selecting premium fabric to applying couture techniques to elevate the modern woman. We believe that what a woman wears influences her mood, confidence and self-expression, and we're here to provide her with beautiful choices.

www.karengee.com

When Karen Gee brought together a group of kind, driven and highly successful women into a community called Global Girls, and I had the privilege of being one of them, I knew instantly that something special had happened.

Not everyone from the group is in the book but you will get to know the essence of the amazing women this elegant leader draws into her space.

Each one of us are proud to be a nearest and dearest to Karen Gee, who is so humble in the impact she makes in the lives of those who have the honour of knowing her.

Karen is a champion for all women and clothes us all in so much more than beautiful dresses. Her Karen Gee brand is well-known for making the woman who wears it stand a little taller, smile a little wider and stand confidently in the power that she is. Karen Gee goes that extra mile for her customers and many of us have the joy of becoming her friend.

So please enjoy and be inspired by the magnificence that is our Global Girls book. It wouldn't be if it were not for the thread that has brough us all together: the wonderful Karen Gee.

With love,

Karen Mc Dermott